May 2012

To Buck
    Thanks for your
help in maintaining
my yard.
            Alice

Cruising Through

Life

A Memoir

ALICE LATIMER

Published by RSE Publishing
403 N. Harper Street, Laurens, SC 29360, U.S.A.

ISBN 978-0-9837103-5-6

Printed in the United States of America
Edited by Amanda L. Capps
Book Design by Michael Seymour
Cover Design by Dan Fowler

Introduction

She is my mother in every sense of the word. To say anything more would diminish the meaning. Her life can be viewed as five phases: her youth, early marriage, her career, retirement with my father, and life after my father's passing. More meaningful than the many places she has visited are the friends and acquaintances she has made. Her memories are sometimes humorous and sometimes tragic, but always enriched by the relationships she has had with others.

James L. Latimer

When my grandfather, Charles Latimer, passed away, I was introduced to feelings of emptiness I knew could not be filled. One such feeling came from knowing I could never introduce my future wife, children, and grandchildren to a man who had had such a great impact on me – who led me on many adventures around the world and taught me many of my earliest lessons.

Sadly, a day will come when I can no longer hug my grandmother, and I will have only memories. I am grateful that my grandma has shared her story in her own words, so that one day, when the world is very different from what it is today, I can share with my future beloveds the story of this extraordinary woman. Reading her story, I have learned many new things, and I can understand how she obtained her values, which were passed down to me.

She is a lady who witnessed the transformation of cultures and values around the world, but one thing is for certain, my grandma will always be my grandma.

Richard Latimer

Around the World in 88 Years

The Americas:
Alaska, Canada, Mexico, St. Pierre & Miquelon, United States (continental), Costa Rica, El Salvador, Guatemala, Honduras, Nicaragua, Panama, San Blas Islands, Argentina, Bolivia, Brazil, Colombia, Ecuador, Peru, Venezuela

Caribbean:
Bahamas, Dominican Republic, Puerto Rico, Virgin Islands (American and British), Antigua, Leeward Islands, St. Kitts & Nevis, Barbados, Martinique, St. Lucia, Aruba, and Trinidad & Tobago

Atlantic Ocean:
Azores Islands, Bermuda, Canary Islands, Greenland, Iceland, and Madeira

Pacific Ocean:
Guam, Hawaiian Islands, Australia, Fiji Islands, New Zealand, Tasmania, Cook Islands, French Polynesia, Galapagos Islands, American Samoa, and Western Samoa

Europe & The Mediterranean:
England, Ireland, Jersey, Scotland, Wales, Denmark, Finland, Norway, Spitsbergen, Sweden, Andorra, Belgium, France, Germany, Gibraltar, Italy, Liechtenstein, Luxembourg, Monaco, Netherlands, Portugal, San Marino, Spain, Switzerland, Vatican City, Albania, Austria, Bosnia & Herzegovina, Croatia, Czech Republic, Greece, Hungary, Macedonia, Montenegro, Poland, Serbia, Slovak, Slovenia, Bulgaria, Estonia, Latvia, Lithuania, Romania, Russia, Turkey, Cyprus, Dodecanese Islands, Ionian Islands, Balearic Islands, Malta, and Sicily

Near East:
Israel and Palestine

Africa:
Egypt, Morocco, Tunisia, Benin, Ghana, Ivory Coast, Senegal, Lesotho, South Africa, Swaziland, and Kenya

Asia:
Turkey, India, Malaysia, Singapore, Thailand, Vietnam, China, Cambodia, Laos, Indonesia, Lesser Sunda Islands, Philippines, Hong Kong, Japan, South Korea, and Macao

Indian Ocean:
Seychelles

Cruising Through Life: A Memoir

I am sitting on the deck of my cruise ship, looking out to the sea. I think of all the interesting people I have met on cruise ships and in many parts of the world. One man from Canada has recently stopped by to chat. He thought Dick and I looked like a couple who had been married for years. We explained we were friends who had lost our mates. I had been married 61 years when Chuck died in September of 2008, and Dick had been married 53 years when Marge died in December of 2003. He wanted to know how we had met, and I explained a mutual friend had gotten us together. Our interviewer thought it great that we were no longer alone and hoped when he got to be our age he wouldn't be either. He told us he had been divorced after 20 years of marriage. He was then alone for eight years before meeting his present wife. He was a salesman who had business with a certain company. When he called to make an appointment, he was asked if he would buy the staff a meal or a beverage. He explained he would buy neither. At this point, the lady with whom he talked said the company would buy him a meal. The woman later became his wife. Life has a way of bringing people together if you're open to possibilities, I suppose.

We had left Miami a day earlier after watching huge

containers being loaded on ships going to distant ports. As I watched these ships, I thought of my own life and my travels to foreign ports. Never for a moment in my youth could I have guessed I would have the travel opportunities that came my way. I thought of my parents' forebears, who ventured from the British Isles in the 1800s. I wonder what circumstances made them come when no family or jobs awaited them. My grandmother, with her brother and two sisters, soon found partners to marry, and they settled down in the area near New York. I suppose that was the beginning of a great adventure for all of us!

And I look forward to another cruise to another destination next year. Where I shall go and whether Dick wants to join me remains to be seen. He has a desire to take a river cruise in Europe, perhaps on the Danube, as there are beautiful cities to be seen. I have never taken an overnight river cruise. Maybe that will be our next trip.

My Ancestors

Mother's Family

My maternal great grandmother and grandfather lived in Rotherhithe, England, where my great grandfather, George Clitter, was a hatter. My understanding is that there was a typhoid epidemic during which everyone in the family got sick except my great grandmother. A four-year-old daughter Katie died. Shortly thereafter, my great grandparents embarked for New York on the S.S. Richmond Hill out of Plymouth, England. They arrived at Ellis Island on June 20, 1887. This was the year before the blizzard of 1888 when snows came up to the second story windows. They settled in a small stone house on Grand Avenue (a Dutch house) in Englewood, NJ. Accompanying them to the U.S. were my grandmother (Alice), her sister (Florence), her sister (Ada), and her brother (George). The family had originally planned to go to British Columbia, but a family by the name of Evans in Englewood suggested that they come look toward America.

Shortly after coming to New Jersey, my grandmother met a widower, 25 years older than she, by the name of Henry Coutant Jackson. He ran a real estate business and sold wallpaper. His wife had died some years earlier, and

George and Eliza Clitter,
maternal great grandparents of Alice Latimer

there were no children. He had a sister, Emma Claude,
who married a man by the name of Reginald Halliday.
There was a dispute in the family over insurance, and to
my knowledge, there was no more contact with Emma
Claude. Mother once pointed out a mansion to me, which
she said belonged to Emma Claude's son who was an
investment banker in New York. At one time, my
grandfather owned a great deal of property on the hill part
of Englewood along the Palisades, which is now very
valuable property. My grandfather also had a brother, John,
who took his place in the Union Army during the Civil
War. I know nothing more about him.

After marriage, my grandparents lived on Knickerbocker Road where my mother (Olive), my aunt (Hilda), and my uncle (Harry) were born. My grandmother had a heart problem as a result of having had rheumatic fever as a child. Since she was sickly, the family had a servant (Josie Van Wagener) who cared for the children. Mother remembered that my grandfather never let any of his children eat meals with my grandmother or him. I know little of my maternal grandfather other than his father had come from England and was reported to have been a teacher in New Rochelle, New York.

Mother recalled a time when someone came into their yard, and my grandfather took his gun and shot out the window at the person. Apparently people took the law

Alice Mary Jackson,
maternal grandmother of Alice Latimer

into their own hands.

Cousin Isabel told me she didn't like Grandfather because she had once seem him shoot his dog in the leg when the dog didn't do something my grandfather wanted.

A favorite story of my mother's was about the Fourth of July when a man with a hand organ and a monkey came into the yard. The monkey was dressed in a little suit and took his hat off to collect coins. Mother was so busy watching him that she put the burning punk too near the firecrackers she was holding, and the firecrackers exploded with a loud bang. The monkey ran up the tree and wouldn't come down. The man got very mad and shouted at the family. Only after some time and with a banana did the monkey come down.

Mother recalled another incident, which happened when they were living at 479 Valley Place. Mother and my aunt went to school at what later became the junior high on Engle Street. The Englewood Hospital was between our home and the school. The hospital kept a flock of goats in the front yard to use for milk for sick babies. On a particular day, there was rain and both my Aunt Hilda and her friend, Marie Bogert, had umbrellas with them. As they passed the hospital, they both started opening and closing the umbrellas while pointing them at the goats. The noise caused the goats to get upset, and the angry herd chased the frightened girls all the way home.

My grandfather died of cancer when my mother was 14. I have no idea how the family managed financially after his death. My mother attended Montclair Normal School and became an elementary teacher. She taught in

Bergenfield and later in Englewood. She recalled going to school in a sleigh in the winter, but I never heard how she got there at other times. She used to say that many of the children, who had recently immigrated, came to school wearing several layers of clothing and that the clothes weren't changed and washed often. The smell got really bad. One teacher sent a child home with a note asking that the child be given a bath and clean clothes. A note came back saying, "Johnny comes to school to be *lernt* not to be *smelt*. He ain't no rose."

Mother's sister, Hilda, became a nurse after attending the St. Luke's Hospital School of Nursing. I think Uncle John (Aunt Florrie's husband) helped with the finances. He may have helped my mother too.

Harry went to work for Coats & Clark in New York when he was either 12 or 14. His job was to sort needles. To my knowledge, he never had education beyond that, but he later became a VP of A.D. Julliard Co. (woolen goods).

Between our house on Valley Place and the Bogerts' home on Engle Street, there was a tennis court or perhaps more than one. Mother, Aunt Hilda, and Uncle Harry belonged to the group who played there along with the Bogerts, the Shepherds, Isabel Snowden, Charles Mauger, Charles Bradley, and probably others whom I don't know. I think my dad met my mother there, but how he came to be invited I don't know.

My dad served in the First World War as a first lieutenant. He served in France near Saint Michel. At one point, his groom was holding the horse's bridle. A shell came and cut the horse in half. Fortunately, Dad wasn't near the horse at the time. When Dad was on his way back to the States, the troop ship he was on was torpedoed just outside the harbor of Brest. The harbor had been closed during the war but was opened for the first time to let the ship in. The ship had a hole the size of a locomotive in its side.

My parents were married at home (Valley Place) on September 11, 1920. I suppose soon after their marriage, they moved to Buffalo, NY, where Dad worked as a salesman for Mobil Oil Co. They lived on Delevan Avenue, and I was born at the Homeopathic Hospital. Mine was a breech birth, and as a result, my right arm was fractured, and the left one had a crack in the bone. I was in a cast for six weeks. Mother said I looked like a piece of raw meat.

We lived in Buffalo until I was four when Mother and I went to Englewood to take care of my grandmother, who was an invalid. She lived until I was seven. I used to carry Grandma's breakfast tray to her and have tea with her.

The day before Christmas in 1930, my grandmother died. I was sent to a neighbor's house to stay until after the funeral. No one then believed a child should attend a funeral. My mother was exhausted after years of caring for Grandma. Mother's sister and her husband lived in Los Angeles just next to Beverly Hills. We were invited to go there for Mother to get a rest. We went by train from New York. I thought it a great adventure to sleep and eat on the train. There were stewards in white jackets who made up our bunks each night and then turned them back to seats during the day.

The scenery too amazed me. I had never before seen farms or fields of corn growing. I especially recall being in Albuquerque, New Mexico, and seeing Indian women with papooses strapped on their backs. The women were dressed in bright colors, which contrasted with their dark hair.

We arrived in Los Angeles, and I started school in Beverly Hills. I wasn't long in school before I came down with mononucleosis. I ran a high fever, which lasted several weeks until an abscess broke in my throat. There was only aspirin to help bring the fever down, and I certainly got a lot of that. Although my aunt was a nurse, she refused to help mother care for me. She feared she'd get my illness. There was no rest for my mother. Mother remarked some time later: "It is a good thing God didn't give Hilda any children."

My only other recollection of our California trip was seeing an Indian man standing at the end of the street directing traffic. He was dressed in Indian clothes and wore feathers on his head. After a number of years, I wondered whether he really existed or whether he existed only in my imagination. My uncle, when questioned, told me I wasn't wrong and that he really did direct traffic. Whether this was his idea or whether he was hired by the city, I don't know.

School days bring a few memories. I remember in my kindergarten room, there was a fish pond and I was intrigued by the fish swimming there. I remember a time one of the boys in my class put my pigtail in the ink well and got ink all over my hair, and then attempted to write with the hair. The boy's sister was secretary to Miss

Griswold, the principal. He was sent to the office and was scolded by his sister. His reply to her was, "Remember what Mother said."

I was always good in writing and got A's in penmanship. My teacher wanted me to learn script writing but I had so much else to do that I never joined the script-writing club.

Dad's Family

My father had one sister, Pearle, who never married. She was an elementary teacher at a public school in lower New York City. Their father was one of a large family. My grandfather was born in Susquehanna, Pennsylvania. When he came to New Jersey, I don't know. He was a butter and

Pearle Whittaker was the sister of Alice Latimer's father. She worked as a school teacher in lower New York City.

egg salesman who, in his later years, lived with my aunt. My only contact with any of my dad's family was to an aunt in Jersey City and two first cousins. His aunt was a teacher who lived to be 100 years old. For some reason, I never saw any of the family except on rare occasions.

My dad's mother, Alice Jane Clarke, died at a young age of a lung condition. I never knew her or heard much about her. Her mother was one of 11 or 12 children brought to Columbia, South Carolina, from Connecticut sometime before the Civil War. They came south by stagecoach. My great grandfather must have been some type of mechanic as he was reported to have worked on the cotton gin.

My great grandmother and her sister married men from Columbia. When the Civil War broke out, the parents returned to the North because they didn't want their sons to fight for the Confederacy. The two girls therefore did not go north, but stayed in Columbia until sometime after the war was over.

My great grandfather's parents ran a stagecoach inn on what is now Route One in Columbia. His ancestors had come in the late 1700s from County Cork, Ireland. They had received a 600-acre land grant from the governor of South Carolina. They were probably Catholic when they arrived, but became Lutheran for lack of a Catholic church. My father tried for years to find out information about the family, but was told all the records of the Civil War times had been destroyed. This turned out to be untrue.

My great grandfather and his brother-in-law served on the Confederate side. I was told that my great grandfather fought in the battle of Fort Sumter. He went home on leave and died with my grandmother in his lap. I have never discovered the cause of his death. As mentioned earlier, the two wives stayed in Columbia during the war. Whether my great grandmother's brother-in-law died in the war, I never have found out.

About 15 years ago, I asked a mutual friend if she would help me find my family. With her help and the help of the local library, I found a Mrs. Clarke who had been doing genealogy on my family. The day I visited her, she took out a large sheet of brown paper and laid it on the floor. She had charted the family from the two brothers who had come from Ireland to the present generation. She showed me my branch of the family and said I had a cousin (now 102 years old) still living in Lexington. There were so many names on the paper that I couldn't copy any but my branch. I said I'd come back at a later time to copy the rest. When I did suggest coming back about a year later, Mrs. Clark said she was too ill to see me. I soon learned she had died. I tried repeatedly to find out whether some other family member had the paper, but no one knew anything about it. Imagine my surprise, when about a year ago, I met a woman who told me this Mrs. Clark had had the paper folded on a table in her kitchen. One day, she decided to thaw some liver for dinner. She laid the liver on the paper to thaw. Apparently she forgot about the meat, because when she checked the liver was thawed and all the blood had run into the paper. She had to throw the paper out. So much for my getting any more information. Incidentally, I did go to see my 102-year-old cousin. She was by then confused and had no idea who I was. Since then, I have met her son, a World War II pilot, and another was cousin. If only my dad had been alive to know I found his family.

Alice Latimer's Birth Certificate: September 22, 1923

Victorian home of Alice Latimer's grandmother in
Englewood, New Jersey

Childhood Memories And Friends

My grandmother's home was built in the Victorian style having been built around 1886. The living room and dining room had white marble fireplaces. The ceilings were 13 feet high. We had a coal furnace, and heat was distributed through registers in the floor. On a cold winter day, one can stand on the register and let the hot air warm you from the bottom to the top. Our kitchen had a coal stove to warm the back of the house, make hot water, and cook much of our food. In winter, we could pop corn in a basket over the coals. My friends enjoyed coming to visit because their houses didn't have coal stoves.

In the back yard was a huge cherry tree. The branches came together towards the bottom, making a rather large shelf. In the days of my youth, we had to use our imaginations to entertain ourselves. Thus, the tree shelf became the counter of a store. My friend, Gertrude, and I spent hours selling sugar, flour, salt, and other staples to each other at our "store." When we tired of this activity, we went to Gertrude's home where she had a swing, which had two seats facing each other on a platform. This became our trolley car, our train, or our car. One of us was the conductor who collected the fare, and the other was the passenger.

Young Alice – always ready to travel – visits the Clitters in New Rochelle, NY.

Other days, we played with our dolls, which were made of rubber and could be washed. We had bassinets that held water. We carried these to each other's houses and spent hours washing, drying, and dressing our dolls.

My three closest friends, other than Gertrude, were Mary Tipping, Helen Mittlacher, and Mary Lou Norton. I believe Mary and Helen started kindergarten with me, and Mary Lou came to Englewood while I was in the second or third grade. We remained close friends all through school, playing together, skating together, and joining Girl Scouts together. Even now, I keep in contact with Helen and Mary Lou. Mary, unfortunately, is no longer living.

Next door to me lived a lad who was a bit older than I. There was a barn behind his house, which held various-sized pieces of lumber. Junior, as I called him, enjoyed building a house for me where we would sit and eat our lunch. I particularly liked chocolate pudding, but it had to have whipped cream on top. Once my mother had no cream. I complained to Junior who offered to remedy the situation. He did so by grating chalk on top. Needless to say, I couldn't eat the pudding, and Junior was in my bad graces.

Young Alice in her favorite dress made by her mother

A Christmas portrait of Alice's family

Family Get Togethers

My family is a small one, as I am an only child. I have two first cousins and three second cousins. It was our custom to get my uncle's family, my cousin's family, and my family together on all the holidays. We rotated, going to one family's house at Christmas, another at New Year's, and the third family at Easter. This custom continued throughout the years.

When I was a child, the George Washington Bridge did not exist. We had to take the Yonkers ferry to cross the Hudson River to get to the New York side where my cousins lived. It was such an adventure to wait in line for the ferry to arrive, put the car on the ferry, and then to wait at the ferry rail for the boats to cross the river. I never tired of watching the boats on the river. I wondered where they were all going.

My great aunt Belle made wonderful blueberry pie. At one of our dinners, my dad was asked if he'd like some pie. He received a piece that he deemed too small. When he complained, he was offered a whole pie. Everyone laughed at his gluttony, but the pie was delicious!

Usually on Sundays, we visited either Aunt Pearle and her friend, Aunt Florence, or we went to my Uncle Harry's home to be with Aunt Rosemary, my cousins, Virginia and Jane, and him. When my dad was home, we took long rides, often as far as Bear Mountain. He enjoyed smoking a cigar, which made the car smell especially bad if the windows were closed. Mother and I would complain loudly.

Mother began doing substitute teaching at Cleveland School, which I attended. Sometimes, I had her as a teacher, and it seemed strange to say "Mother" when I wanted something. At that time, she took classes at Teachers College in New York. I then went across the street to stay with Mrs. Mabee. She was an elderly lady who wore long dresses and bonnets. She was an excellent cook, and I enjoyed her meals. She also had a beautiful garden with hollyhocks, roses, poppies, and delphinium. I learned my gardening skills from her.

Mr. Stagg lived just across from us. There was a sidewalk that went all around his house. This is where I wanted to roller skate, as I could go round and round. I guess I must have driven him crazy with the noise, but I don't ever remember him telling me to stop. He'd sit on the front porch and rock. One day he said: "Don't know what the world is coming to. The bathing suits get shorter and shorter."

Not far from my house was a store that sold papers and magazines and had an ice cream bar. One could get a soda, a sundae, a cone, or a quart of Breyer's ice cream. The couple who ran the store were Elsie and Harry Maxwell. When Elsie filled the quart container with the ice cream, she made sure she didn't give more than a quart. Harry on the other hand, would get to talking and pile in the ice cream. I always hoped to get Harry to serve me.

Another store I'd frequent was the butcher shop. Mr. Klinkelstein was the owner. His daughter, Alice, was in my class. Before I left his store with my purchase, he'd ask if I'd like a piece of bologna. When I agreed I would like some, he'd take out a roll of bologna and cut off a hunk for me. I'd leave the store happily chewing.

Hard Times

I was six years old when the stock market plunged, and many people lost all the savings they had. This happened to my uncle's father-in-law. My uncle bought his house and added an apartment so his father and mother-in-law would have a place to live.

My dad lost his job, and for a while, he did not work. Mother and I continued to live in my grandmother's house. Dad lived in Detroit. Later, Dad got a job as a book salesman. His territory was Chicago to Los Angeles. Mother would never leave Englewood. We didn't see my dad for nearly five years. He later came back to live with us, but he travelled eight months of the year. There were bread lines in our city for people needing food despite the fact bread cost 10 cents a loaf. Women went begging door to door for canned food. One woman got some cans from my mother, but apparently, she didn't like them. She went around the corner to my aunt's house and offered to sell them to her. I wasn't particularly affected by the Depression. Mother and my Aunt Pearle made sure I got what I needed or wanted. Mother made all my dresses, which she hand smocked. The one dress I liked the most was of robin's egg blue crepe de chine smocked with pink rosebuds. It was trimmed around the neck and armholes with lace. A cousin of my age died when I was about nine years old. I received all her ready-made clothes, which I thought was something special.

My Aunt Aida lived around the corner. She was really my great aunt. She and my uncle Weg had a large house. Their only son had been killed in an auto accident. I spent a great deal of time there, especially if my mother and I had a disagreement over something. I'd march off to my aunt's home and unload my feelings. She'd listen and then suggest we have some sugar cookies and Cott's raspberry soda. After the cookies and soda and a stint in her rocking chair, everything seemed to get solved.

Polio

The summer before I was 10 years old, I went to Madison, Connecticut, with my aunt Pearle for vacation. I don't know whether it was there or at home that I contracted polio. I began school in the fall, but in October, I had terrible headaches and fever. The pediatrician was called. He came to our house where he did a spinal tap and declared I had polio.

I was taken by ambulance to the county hospital, which was a distance from our home. Mother didn't drive and would not have been able to visit me. Our kind doctor said he'd pick Mother up each afternoon when he went to check on me and would take her to the hospital. He kept this up the entire time I was in the hospital. The only thing I remember of my hospital stay was that I got cold Cream of Wheat for breakfast. To this day, I can't stand that type of cereal.

After I left the hospital, Mother and I went to Uncle Harry's house to stay. He was alone at the time and glad to have the company, as his wife and children were in Florida for the winter. His house was all on one level, which made it easier for Mother. I made my way around by being pulled in a red wagon on which my uncle had placed a board. I enjoyed being with my uncle because he had an English setter named Jerry who kept us amused. One time, he found a carton with a dozen eggs at someone's door and brought the carton home in his mouth. He deposited the contents in a hole in the ground right outside the front door. We tried to track down the owner of the eggs to no avail. The angel cake and gold cake we made with those eggs were a great treat.

As I think back to the time I had polio, I recall how helpless I felt. For a time, I couldn't sit up or walk. One time, there was a noise coming from my wastebasket. I called my mother to see what was causing the sound. At first, she thought I was kidding her, but when she finally came and looked, she saw a mouse. It was not certain that I would ever walk again. I was determined that I would get out of bed and walk. I certainly learned patience from having this disease, and my strong will to stay active and healthy remains with me to this day.

As I got better, it was suggested I be sent to Warm Springs, Georgia, for therapy. Mother didn't want me to go so far away, and the doctor then suggested that the physical therapist from the hospital come and demonstrate how to give me salt baths in our bathtub. Rock salt was dissolved in hot water into which I was placed. A neighbor came and helped mother put me in the tub. After about a half hour spent moving my legs, I was taken out of the water and massaged with cocoa butter. To this day, the smell of cocoa butter reminds me of this time.

I was out of school an entire year, which would have been difficult for me had I not had Mother and Aunt Pearle as teachers. Both worked with me to get my math skills up to par. I believe my teachers at school must have sent assignments home too as I was able to pass on to sixth grade in the fall.

I attended Englewood Junior High. I went by trolley because it was a long walk. The school building had formerly been the high school that my mother had attended. In high school, our drama teacher was Mrs. Travolta, mother of movie star John Travolta. Bruce Forbes, brother of Steve Forbes, was in my class. His dad was a New York investment broker and was on the local school board. We had a French teacher who took our class to New York to visit the ship Normandy. In those days, people could go aboard ships. I remember we ate frog legs and cream puffs (a strange combination), but we were all thrilled to be on such a luxurious ship. I never thought then I'd be traveling by ship to many parts of the world. Each Friday, we attended an assembly where we had speakers who told us about different topics. Two of the speakers were from the Museum of Natural History in New York and were fathers of my classmates. There was an advantage to living near The Big Apple.

During warm weather, Mother and I took many walks together, especially in the hill section of Englewood, which in those days was not terribly developed. Then one Sunday afternoon, we passed two young women pushing a carriage with a baby inside. There were two police dogs, one on either side of the carriage. We realized that this was the Lindbergh baby, who was later kidnapped and murdered.

Another classmate, Betty Guy, had a father who worked for RCA. In our home economics class one day, she told us they had a little black box at home that had a screen in front. They could turn a dial and could see people talking. We all wondered whether she was just making up a story, but we later realized this was the beginning of TV. The programs could be produced in New York and transmitted to Englewood, which was just across the Hudson River. Before we had TV, I used to listen to programs on the radio. I particularly liked Buck Rogers because he was able to leave planet Earth. My mother thought it was just a lot of nonsense because everyone knew you couldn't get off this planet. She never lived to see a man land on the moon or to talk on a telephone via satellite, something that is now part of her grandson's profession.

After finishing junior high, I attended Dwight Morrow High School. The school was in Tudor style and one story high. In warm weather we had our classes outside on the lawn. I was in the classical curriculum, meaning that I studied French, Latin, social studies, English, biology,

Dorothy Lingner and Helen Mittlacher Erickson with another high school friend at a reunion for Dwight Morrow High School (Englewood, NJ) where Alice graduated in 1941

40

chemistry, and algebra. Girls in those days weren't encouraged to take analysis, calculus, or physics. It was thought only boys needed those courses. Our physical education course included ice skating in the winter because there was a lake behind the school.

In my senior year, I began to date. My first boyfriend was in college studying "pre-med." He later attended Jefferson Medical School. I wore his fraternity pin, and together, we attended many of the college dances. The romance lasted until I went to college.

Another advantage of living near New York was that we could attend performances at the Metropolitan opera. I heard Laurence Tibbett and Lily Pons sing, as well as the other well-known singers of that day. My classmates and I went on Saturday afternoons with our music teacher who told us the plot of each opera. The opera I must remember was "Lohengrin." In the opera, Lohengrin appears on a boat drawn by a swan. He is standing erect and is in shining armor. The sight of the knight with the accompanying music is something I can picture to this day.

Our foreign policy club attended foreign policy meetings held at the Hotel Taft. These excursions into New York gave us the opportunity to hear debates among the political leaders of the 1930s. Eleanor Roosevelt and Adlai Stevenson were among the speakers. I remember being especially impressed by Eleanor Roosevelt because she could speak so eloquently.

Alice, third from right, is pictured with friends from
Simmons College in Boston.

College Days

I had decided to study home economics in order to become a dietician. My great aunt Belle had opened the first cafeteria for the telephone company in Chicago. Hearing about her work made me think I might enjoy the same profession.

My life really began when I went away to college. I had originally planned to go to Rutgers University because, as a state university, it was cheaper. My dad had heard of a small woman's college in Boston named Simmons College. The school had a good reputation and offered a degree in home economics, which I wanted. I applied and was offered a scholarship. Getting the scholarship meant I could afford to go there. Tuition, room and board ran about $1,000.00 a year, a great difference from today's cost.

I can't remember now whether I took the train from New York to get there or whether my folks drove me. I know I wore my new plaid wool suit although the temperature was near 80 degrees. I was assigned to a large residence in Brookline, Massachusetts. My roommate had attended a private girls school where she had had no contact with boys. Living with her proved to be a great problem for me and made me decide I'd never want a roommate again. Every weekend, she would go out to one of the men's colleges and get drunk. She would come back in such a state that other girls would have to undress her and put her to bed. Since I didn't drink and her friends were not my friends, I often was shut out of our room. I remember at exam time, I found her studying while propped up in bed with her book upside down. Fortunately for me, she left after the first semester.

College Friends

Living on campus at the college gave me the opportunity to make many friends. My crowd included Elaine Snyder, Dorothy Forrester, Natalie Chisholm, Marjorie Vail, Phyllis Barnau, and Louise Seki. Phyllis studied business and became the private secretary to John Foster Dulles and Dean Rusk (both secretaries of state). She later married Bill Macomber who served as the U.S. Ambassador to Turkey.

Louise came from Washington State. Her father had owned a large vegetable farm. Louise's mother and father were born in Japan, but Louise was born in the States. By the time the Second World War began, her parents were dead. At this time, the Japanese were being put in internment camps, and Louise would have been put in one except the Quakers stepped in and sent her to my college on the East Coast. She had no family to visit on holidays, and once came home with me. We became friends and have remained so over the years. She married a man from England, Derek Hoare, and lived there while we were in Germany. She later lived in Texas while her husband was a professor at the University of Texas. He died tragically, and Louise and her son moved to Los Angeles where she became a professor at UCLA. She was a great friend to Jim while he was at Caltech and remained so after he married and lived in the L.A. area.

Meeting Interesting People

Because I was a home economics major, I was sometimes asked to go to a home where help was needed for a party. One home was in Brookline where the host was an agent for musicians. The first time I went, he was entertaining the Trapp family. I remember the small son kept talking while the group sang. His mother finally came over and told him to take a key and lock his lips. The second time I went to the home, Marion Anderson was the guest. I thought her voice was beautiful. At that party, I got sick and had to leave early. I called for two of my friends to come and finish cleaning up.

Another time, I went to Beacon Hill for an afternoon tea. The house had a room about two stories tall with a balcony around it. A grand piano was in the middle of the room and two tall candlesticks were nearby. The house was freezing. I guess she kept the heat down due to fuel costs. I was to say to the guests: "It is a bit chilly in the house. If you wish to leave your coats on, you may." The guests arrived in minks and sables. When I told them they could leave their coats on, one lady said, "My dear, it's always freezing in here."

Dean Mesick (Dean of Simmons College) was on the board of directors of Mt. Holyoke College. One Saturday, she was to go there for a board meeting. The lady I just mentioned invited her for breakfast. As our dean was leaving, she was told there was a bag of goodies for her to take with her. When the bag was opened, it contained two Tootsie Rolls, some peppermints, and one lollipop. I smile as I think of Dean Mesick, a dignified lady, driving along, sucking a lollipop.

On a Sunday afternoon in December, my fellow housemates and I were sitting in the dorm living room having a demitasse and mints when news came over the radio that Pearl Harbor had been attacked. We all sat stunned because we realized our boyfriends would be called to fight. I had met a boy from Tufts University who was studying engineering. He joined the Navy at the end of the year and served in the Pacific theater. The only males who were left for us were in the ROTC programs. We girls kept ourselves entertained on weekends by going to the theater or going to free concerts, which were held at the various museums. Going to religious group meetings was also an option, and I chose Westminster House, which was associated with the Presbyterian church. My senior year, I became president of our group at Westminster House, a Presbyterian youth center. We had meetings Sunday afternoon with supper. This group also held Sunday services at the chapel of the Episcopal seminary in Cambridge. We students ran the service with each one having a specific task. It was during this time that I met a medical student from Harvard. I grew very fond of him and was disappointed when he graduated and I never heard from him again. I later learned he was engaged to a Radcliffe graduate the whole time we were dating.

During my senior year in college, I was required to do field work for my course in Institutional Management. I had to leave my dorm at 4 a.m. in order to get to whatever facility I was assigned to. I had to dress with a hat and gloves to look professional. It was often dark when I started out, and I was often alone. I was never approached by a stranger, but a friend was, and she ran back to the dorm terrified. Her dad complained to the administration, and the practice of early assignments stopped.

Our graduation was held in June of 1945 at Symphony Hall. In August of the same year, I started an internship at Presbyterian Hospital in New York City. The internship was extremely taxing. Since it was just after the end of the war, we were extremely short of staff. I lived at the hospital and worked split shifts. I went on duty at 6 a.m. and worked until 10 a.m. I was off for two hours and went back to work from noon until 2 p.m. I was off 2-4 p.m. and worked 4-6 p.m. We had to make sure the patients got the foods they were supposed to have according to their diets. After meals were served, we had to check the patients' charts to see if changes had to be made. We then had to visit the patients to see if they had any desires or complaints. Since we were short of help, we often had to wash dishes to have them ready for the next meal. After eating our evening meal, we took the subway downtown to Columbia University to take courses towards a master's degree.

The director for our program was a "Miss" Ross. I found out later that her husband was in the hospital at the time. She was very strict. We weren't supposed to talk to or date any intern. We were also supposed to take courses at Columbia University in the evenings, often getting home at 11 p.m. I got so tired and discouraged; I decided I would quit the program. I told this to "Miss" Ross who said if I did she would blackball me from the profession for life. I went home in the afternoon and told my mother what had happened. She didn't say anything until the next morning when she asked me what I planned to do now that I had decided to give up the internship. I stated I had decided to stay and finish. Several years later, after I had married, gone back to New York, and was working at Columbia University, I met "Miss" Ross who asked why I hadn't asked her for a job. I never told her that her earlier remarks to me had made me decide I would never again work for her and that my experience with hospital work would keep me away from it for many years.

One funny thing that I do remember from my hospital days was the hot summer night when I ordered a glass of iced tea and the young girl on duty at the cafeteria brought me a glass of iced water with a tea bag floating on the top. I was distressed by a patient only one time. We had a patient who had had his nose and ears blown off in a war accident. His face was terribly disfigured. He came into my office, which had a single light bulb hanging from the ceiling. The light shone on his face, and as I looked at him, I felt I'd either faint or vomit. I had to make the excuse that a patient needed to see me immediately and I hurried out of the office. I don't know if he realized how upset I had been.

I got viral pneumonia before the end of my internship and had to stay another month, but I had completed its demands. After leaving the hospital, I returned to Boston area where I had been offered a job as nutritionist for Roxbury Neighborhood House. This was a recreation center in the slums of Roxbury. The people who used the center were mostly Irish or Italian. Many lived in cold water flats. I held cooking classes for the children. I hated rainy days because we had to close the windows and the smell of unwashed children almost made me vomit. I learned to walk on the edge of the curb when I walked home from the subway because I didn't want anyone to grab me from a doorway. Fortunately, the people in the neighborhood knew me, and no one ever bothered me.

While I was still at the hospital, I became engaged to the Tufts student who was then in the Navy stationed in Hawaii. About the time I went to the neighborhood house, he returned to Boston. Things went along well between us until one night when we had been out and it was late. Since he didn't want to go with me to my residence, I said I'd take a taxi. He told me I needed to save money for when we married, and I should walk home. I decided then and there that if he didn't care any more about my safety than that, I wasn't going to marry him. I returned the ring to him.

A few months later, one of the ministers at Westminster House came to me and said the following Sunday there was to be a meeting for graduate students, and he wanted me to be the hostess. These were veterans returning on the GI Bill. I agreed to go and found I was the only female among 15 males. It was there I met Chuck, who in just a few months would become my husband.

Chuck and Alice Latimer on their wedding day,
September 7, 1947, in Tenafly, NJ

Marriage

Chuck and I met on a Sunday evening in March of 1947, at Westminster House in Boston. One of the fellows (who had a red Buick convertible) asked to take me home, as he wanted to see a settlement house. Chuck asked if he could come along – under the pretense that he too wanted to see the house. They both took me home. Within an hour, Chuck called me and asked me for a date. We saw each other regularly after that. Chuck didn't have a car when we met, but shortly thereafter, he bought one. He had missed the last subway home one evening and had to take several buses to get there. It took almost all night for him to reach his boarding house.

Chuck and I courted throughout the spring while I was serving as a nutritionist at the Roxbury Neighborhood House, and later, when I was at the Boston YWCA and Green Mountain Camp as director. Mrs. Gamble, I think, arranged for this. I reported to the camp April 1, and stayed with a farmer and his wife, Arvid Anderson and Martha. They lived in an eighteenth century home. I ate my breakfast sitting by a large fireplace. Martha's pancakes with lingonberries were outstanding. Later, I stayed with Carroll and Lelia Williams in Westminster, Vermont. Spring always brought fresh asparagus, homemade rye bread, and freshly

Alice and Chuck Latimer are pictured with her parents, J. Rowland and Olive Whittaker.

churned butter. Carroll taught me to drive and enjoyed telling me the jokes he had learn at the cattle auctions.

Chuck and I had not planned to see each other for a couple of months. I guess he missed me because he arrived at camp the first weekend I was there and each weekend thereafter. Memorial Day weekend, I went to New Jersey (my home). Chuck came after midnight. I had told him how to reach my home by counting stoplights. I didn't know the lights were shut off at midnight or that he would arrive late. He had to follow a bus, which stopped at the corner of my street.

He stayed with George Willard, the camp caretaker. George was a real Vermonter. He married a young girl who died within a few months after they married. When I told him how sorry I was, he said, "Yep, I lost my wife and two good hound dogs all at the same time."

Chuck proposed to me at the camp. We planned to marry in December. In August, Chuck called to say he had bought a two-family house, and he figured we should marry during his summer break. I should mention that Chuck saw an ad in the paper about the house. The price was $5,500.00 – too good to be true since the address given in the ad was in an area of more expensive houses. Actually, it was the address of the owner. Chuck borrowed $5,000.00 from the Reliance Cooperative Bank and used a $500.00 war bond to pay for the house. The owner knew the people at the bank and arranged for us to get a loan with four percent interest.

I called Mother and told her to sit down. I then told her I planned to marry in one month. She didn't think it was possible, but it worked out. We were married September 7, 1947, in the Tenafly Presbyterian Church with a reception at The Englewood Women's Club. I wore a white satin dress with a sweetheart neckline and a train. I borrowed Marjorie Vail's veil and carried a bouquet of white chrysanthemums with a white orchid in the center. Marge Vail (a college friend) was my maid of honor, and my cousins Virginia and Jane Jackson and Virginia Mauger were bridesmaids. Chuck's parents didn't attend our wedding because he was marrying a Yankee. His brother did and was Chuck's best man. In later years, this Yankee was the one who cared for Chuck's parents, and we all loved each other. We spent the first night in Newark at the Robert Trent Hotel. The day of the wedding the temperature was over 90, and there was no air conditioning, so Mother and a friend powdered my body to help me get the dress on. I wore a brown faille two-piece suit to go away in and took the orchid from the bouquet to wear on the suit. It really was too hot for such an outfit, but I was too excited to realize that.

After our wedding and honeymoon in Williamsburg and South Carolina, we moved into our little house in Cambridge. Chick had a semester at Harvard Law School before attending the Harvard School of Education. At night, he and worked at a bakery as a bookkeeper. I worked as the nutritionist at the YWCA; I had changed jobs. Our neighborhood had some interesting residents. Our next-door neighbors were Italian. Once a month, at about 4 a.m., they'd get into a fight and scream at each other. After the husband went to work, his wife would go to the back door and throw some of her dishes down on the cement to break.

Our upstairs neighbors were an Irish mother and daughter, the Ryans. One day, when I returned home from work, I found a package tied to my doorknob. I carried the package into our living room and placed it on the sofa. The package moved, and I thought there might be a baby inside. When I opened the package, I found a hen. A friend of Chuck's who was leaving town had given it to us. The neighbors next door lent us their cat carrier, and I put the chicken in it. For a week, I kept the chicken in our basement and fed it oatmeal. At the end of the week, I asked Chuck to kill the bird so I could make a chicken pie. He took the chicken to the back yard and wrung its

Chuck Latimer's parents, Charles and Annie Mae Latimer

head off. The hen was still moving. In a short time, I had a call from Elizabeth Ryan, asking me to check on her mother. Mrs. Ryan thought she must have been hallucinating because she had looked out the window and seen a live chicken. Later, she saw a headless chicken flopping about. I explained we were about to have chicken pie.

We had a lot of snow and ice in winter. Our garage, which we rented, was a block from the house. One snowy and icy day, Chuck went to get our car. As he drove the car out of the garage, it got stuck in the snow, and the wheels just spun around. Chuck tried for several minutes to get the car unstuck. A burly man then appeared and ordered him out of the car. He rocked the car backwards and forwards and then put on speed and got the car unstuck. It turned out he was a truck driver. His parting words to Chuck were: "If I'd known you weren't my neighbor I'd have come out sooner."

The principal at the Edward Devotion School where Chuck taught was Don Lytle. He was extremely formal at school, but come Friday night, he'd kick up his heels. Each Friday after work, I'd stop by the store and buy lobster for our dinner. At that time, lobsters cost 49 cents a pound and weighed about one pound. On weeknights, Chuck and Don ate dinner together because I worked until 9 p.m. Fridays, Don would ask Chuck where he planned to eat dinner, and Chuck would always invite Don to eat with us.

Looking through an old photo album, I found pictures of Green Mountain Camp in West Dummerston, Vermont. As I mentioned, before I married, and while I lived in Cambridge, I worked six months of the year at the YMCA and was camp director in Vermont for the other six months. We kept our house in Cambridge, but while in Vermont, we lived in a little house that had been a school belonging to the camp. It was on the river with a covered bridge nearby.

We had a goat as a pet, and we took him with us in the car as we drove around. The goat followed me everywhere. We also had three pet skunks (babies without any scent), Jinkle, Tinkle, and Dinkle.

There had been trouble with boys from Brattleboro bringing a cannon nearby and setting it off to scare the campers. One night, as we were going to bed, we heard a sound and thought the boys had come back. Chuck put on his clothes and shoes, but he didn't tie them. He grabbed an axe and ran out of the house, down the road towards the bridge. I shouted, "Be careful; don't hurt them!" He lost his shoes along the way. A car came across the bridge driven by an old lady who asked, "Doctor Latimer, where are you going?" He explained, and she then brought him back home after stopping to get his shoes. We never found out who she was.

Other neighbors in Cambridge were Alec and Maisie Smart. They were from Arbroath, Scotland. Alec worked at M.I.T. When we moved into our house, they came over to visit. Masie looked around and saw no furniture, as it was impossible to buy new furniture after the war. All our sheets and blankets were spread on the floor for a bed and a coffee table and trunk served us as table and chairs. Masie insisted on our sleeping at their house until we could get better furniture. She carried over a table and chairs, and we did sleep in their guest room for several weeks until I insisted we must sleep in our house. At that time, we brought the bed to our house. How lucky we were to have found such caring neighbors. Many years later when they had returned to Scotland and built a house, we paid them a surprise visit and recalled fond memories.

Alice Latimer teaching a soldier in Germany

Beginning Our Careers

Ernest and Ellen Caverly really became our second parents. Dr. Caverly was the superintendent of the Brookline schools. After Chuck got his master's degree, which enabled him to teach social studies, he was hired by the Brookline schools as a social studies teacher at Edward Devotion School. Mr. Caverly had arranged for him to do practice teaching in the Brookline schools. Chuck later got a second master's degree in psychology. We were often invited to the Caverly's for dinner or to go with them to a restaurant. Their daughter lived in Michigan and didn't get home often. I think we took her place in Massachusetts. This friendship kept up over the years, and they visited us in Germany, Panama, and South Carolina. Chuck was asked to represent the schools in matters pertaining to intergroup relations. After two years, it seemed best for him to go to Teachers College, Columbia University and get his doctorate. Temple Israel Brotherhood and the school provided money for us to go. We started at Teachers College in the fall of 1950. I was given the job of managing Horace Mann Cafeteria and doing catering. I also finished my master's degree in Institutional Management. President Eisenhower was at the college in those days. We served about 500 people for lunch each weekday. I had in the cafeteria a Radar Range (an early version of the microwave oven). The people passing through the cafeteria line were amazed I could cook an eight-pound block of frozen peas in just a few minutes.

We lived in Fort Lee, New Jersey, in an apartment Teachers College had rented for graduate students. We were near my parents. We made good friends of the other students and had many pajama parties. This was the time of the Cold War, and it was thought the Russians might bomb New York. A fellow student wanted us to build a bomb shelter in the apartment's front yard. One night about 2 a.m., the air raid sirens went off. We jumped out of bed and ran to the window to see what was going on. All was quiet. I stayed up all the rest of the night just shivering with fright. It was a false alarm. I think of that today whenever I get in a frightening situation.

After completing our degrees in 1951, we returned to the Boston area. We sold our Cambridge house for more than we paid for it and bought a big house on Jordan Road in Brookline. Chuck became a social studies teacher at the Brookline High School, and I ran the cafeteria and taught two cooking classes. I became pregnant in the summer and had to stop my teaching job the second semester. I did, however, work in the evenings as director of the evening adult education program.

Mother came to stay with us after Jim's birth. She would go down to the cellar to wash our clothes, as we had no washing machine. One day, she screamed and came back upstairs. A rat had run between her legs. A few months before, I'd found a rat drowned in our first floor toilet. I accused Chuck of trying to play a trick on me. Of course, he hadn't been playing any trick. It turned out the sewer cap had not been made of metal, as it should have been. A wooden plug had been used instead. Chuck took his .22 caliber rifle and peppered the rat. Our neighbor remarked that he was glad Chuck hadn't shot him because he was such a good shot.

Next door to our Jordan Road home lived Ruth and Harry Rosenfield. Harry owned a diaper washing business. They were wonderful neighbors. After Jim's birth, they gave us a year's diaper service as a gift. In addition, Ruth insisted I use their washer and dryer whenever I needed to wash. I felt I needed to do something in return and therefore agreed to keep their daughter Billie whenever they wanted a vacation.

Early in that year, Dr. Caverly, called to ask if we'd board a Jewish girl from Marshfield whose parents wanted her to attend a school where there were Jewish students. We agreed, and Reina came to live with us. We all got along well. Dr. Caverly knew we had a big house and could use some extra cash. At the time of her birthday, we offered to take her out to dinner. She declined saying we were too old to take her out. We were then about 30 years old. She later went to Simmons, and we still hear from her.

At the time Jim was born, March 15, 1952, little was known about the Rh factor, which causes few problems for newborn babies today. A vaccine is given to pregnant women when there is an incompatibility with her baby's blood. During the time I had polio, I had been given blood from a young woman who had recovered completely from the disease. Doctors assumed I would be less likely to have paralysis if I were given her blood. Unfortunately, she had Rh positive blood, and mine is Rh negative. I already had antibodies before Jim was conceived. During Jim's time in the womb, my blood titers had built up because Jim's blood is Rh positive as was his dad's. As a result of this, Jim's red blood cells were being destroyed. Fortunately, Jim was born in Boston where Dr. Louis Diamond at Children's Hospital had begun treating this condition with exchange transfusions. Blood was taken from the placenta, and fresh blood from a female donor was put in. The procedure continued until all the donated blood had been used. Jim needed only one transfusion to offset the jaundice, which was beginning to appear. The treatment worked, and he is fine today.

Our house on Jordan Road overlooked Cambridge. The first tenants were Catholic. The wife had TB. The husband, an architect, had built a sun porch on the back so she could sleep with lots of air. There was a niche over the fireplace in the living room where a Madonna had been. The next tenants were Jewish and there was a Mezuzah by the front door. The neighbors wondered what we would add. We laughed and said, "Just our family."

In 1953, after two years in Brookline, we moved to Wallingford, Connecticut, where Chuck became vice principal of Lyman Hall High School. Mother and Dad would drive up occasionally to spend a few days. I always kept homemade chicken pies and asparagus in the freezer, which I could pull out at a moment's notice. A funny thing happened there. Jim used to play with Brenda Nye. The

Nyes had a big dog. We had gotten a bag of pecans in the shell. Jim apparently wanted some of them. I happened to look to see what they were doing. Jim was putting a nut into the dog's mouth. The dog would bite it and break the shell. Jim would then remove the nut, and he and Brenda could eat the nut meat.

In 1955, our next move was to Upper Montclair, New Jersey, where Chuck became vice principal of Montclair High School. We lived just a block from Montclair State Teachers College where my mother had gotten her teacher training. It was here that my daughter, Mary, was born on July 14, 1956. The hospital did not have the equipment that Children's Hospital in Boston had nor did our pediatrician have the skill of Dr. Allen. Mary was extremely jaundiced when she was born. She was given three exchange transfusions in four days and lived, but required a great deal of care. I spent much time just feeding her because she had difficulty swallowing. Jim helped by turning Mary so she wouldn't always be in one position. He also ran errands for me. Mother and Dad came often to help out. As a result of anoxia, Mary is mentally handicapped today. She has such a sense of humor, I often wonder what she would have been like had that not happened.

We sent Jim to a wonderful preschool. The director was a pianist who played pieces written by Mozart, Bach, and other noted composers for the children. I believe Jim got his love of music from this remarkable woman.

Summers were very hot in New Jersey, and we had no air conditioning. There was a neighborhood pool behind our house, which helped us keep cool. We'd swim in late afternoon, and then I'd get dinner while wearing my wet bathing suit. Being wet kept me cool.

Beginning Life In Germany – Europe, Our Home For Five Years

In September of 1957, we sailed from New York on the S.S. America for Bremerhaven, Germany, where Chuck was to become the instructional services director with the Dependents Education Group in charge of the Army schools in Germany, France, Italy, and Ethiopia.

We enjoyed our ocean voyage. It was our tenth anniversary, and we were starting on a new path in our life's journey. My mother was upset that we were leaving the States. She had never left Englewood where she had been born even though my dad's territory was from Chicago west to California. Mother told me when I left, I wouldn't see her again alive.

The Latimers in 1957 on the S.S. America en route to Germany

Our trip to Germany was delightful. We sailed on the America from New York amidst a flutter of confetti and friends waving "Good-bye!" This was the time before cruise ships, but there was an orchestra on board and wonderful food. I celebrated my birthday with a cake decorated with marzipan frosting. I was disappointed I didn't have enough space to carry it off the ship. Jim enjoyed playing with other children on the ship and having his own deck chair.

When we reached Bremerhaven and the ship docked, Chuck had forms to complete. Meanwhile, a Red Cross nurse appeared and took Mary from my arms. I didn't want to lose sight of Chuck, but I hurried after her, as I didn't want to be separated from Mary. We got on a nearby train. Every seat was filled, and we were discouraged as we walked up and down, getting more and more tired. Finally we spotted an empty compartment and found seats there. Throughout our journey, a conductor came in and appeared to scold us. We realized we weren't supposed to be there, but we felt we had no other choice. Later, when we understood German, we realized we had sat in a compartment reserved for German persons wounded in World War II. Not understanding a language can put one at a disadvantage.

Our arrival in Karlsruhe was the occasion for a large gathering of officials. We learned there had been a group to meet us in Bremerhaven, but we had missed them. Furthermore, we had not found the part of the train where we were supposed to ride. A whole section, nearly empty, was reserved for Americans. Everyone present was afraid we hadn't gotten to Germany and was happy to see us. We

Chuck and Alice Latimer aboard the S.S. America in 1957

were taken to a temporary apartment on base, which was partially furnished and would suffice until our own furniture arrived.

Our first apartment was off base on the first floor of a two-family house. Our upstairs neighbors were the Aurisches. Herr Aurisch worked for Hinkel Fabrik. We had a coal furnace. Each night, the fire would go out, and in the morning after Chuck went to work, I'd have to go to the basement and try to get the fire started again. Frau Aurisch would hear me trying to chop wood and would come down to help. She spoke no English, and thus my German lessons began. She'd hold up a piece of wood, which was needed to start the coal fire, and say, "Das ist Holz." We progressed to talking about furniture, daily activities, or food. Gradually, the words began to get into my vocabulary. I've found learning a language is like making a snowball. At first, the ball is small but as more snow is applied, it gets bigger and bigger.

Jim went to German kindergarten at this time. The school was run by nuns whose habits included ankle length black dresses and white starched hats that reminded me of windmills. One sister would ride Jim home on the handlebars of her bike. I can still see her coming with her hat flapping in the breeze.

After Jim returned from school, we'd put Mary in her stroller and take a walk. We always passed a German bakery with luscious looking cookies in the window. We'd stop in to buy a huge spritz cookie which we happily ate as we walked along. To this day, spritz cookies are Jim's favorite kind.

We subsequently lived on Luisenstrasse in the downtown area of Karlsruhe. I don't recall much about living there. We had no wonderful neighbors like the Auriches. I clearly remember looking out of our windows at bombed out buildings, which seemed to be surrounding us. At that time, the city hadn't been fully rebuilt.

The Dependents Education Group was a close-knit group headed by Col. John and Mrs. Gwen Steele. Since we were far from home, we had to help one another. We had regular parties when the men tended to stay in the living room, and the women gathered in a bedroom and sat on the bed. If someone had to leave for the States on an emergency, another family would keep the children. We kept two girls for about a month while their mother was in the States caring for her mother. I nursed one of the girls, Cathy, after she came down with scarlet fever.

A weekend in Berchtesgaden

Herr and Frau Pils, who helped Alice learn German

Henny, a friend from Germany, visiting Greenville, SC

Social Activities

I became a member of the German-American Club, which also included French women. Through this club, I met Frau Pils, Frau Birkmann, Frau Heimann, Frau Tröeger, Frau Schultz, and Madam Gazaigne. They were all well educated women who were interested in making friends and learning about the customs of other cultures. We met monthly for the afternoon either at a member's home or at the Officers' Club. There were also parties to which the husbands were invited.

Frau Tröeger had a tale to tell. Her husband was an engineer. They had lived in East Berlin and had been captured by the Russians who forced Dr. Tröeger to work for them. They wanted to escape to the West. Each day, Frau Tröeger would take her children and a picnic basket filled with their lunch and some of her Meissen china to West Berlin. When Russian guards questioned her, she told them she was taking the children on a picnic. They would then let her cross into West Berlin. Once there, she left her china behind, had a picnic, and then returned to the East. Where she left her china, I never learned, but she managed to get it all out before they escaped to the west. After Frau Pils and I got acquainted, we found we had a mutual interest to learn each other's language. She suggested we should get together twice a week. One day we would only speak German, and one day, only English. We did this for several years and both improved our language skills. She later became a marriage counselor for her Catholic church.

Frau Birkmann was the wife of the director of the Karlsruhe Zoo. She and her husband became some of our best friends with whom we spent many evenings. When we went to their apartment, we always found some unusual pets. One time, they had a bush baby, which would cling to the wall by using the suction cups on its feet wet by its urine. It jumped on me, and I had to go and wash my arm. Another time, they had a pig whose low stomach swung as it walked. Herr Dr. Berkman used to love to tease his wife by telling her that his years in an American prisoner of war camp were among the happiest in his life. She would reply with something like, "You shouldn't say that, Karl!" He'd then say, "Henny, it was the only time I could read all day with no one to bother me."

Karl had told us he hadn't been able to go on his honeymoon because a female lion had to have an emergency caesarian section to deliver her cubs. There was no incubator, so he went to bed to keep the cubs warm. I don't think Henny ever forgave him.

Herr Dr. Professor Schulz was a professor at the technical university. He was a very proper German. Years later, when we returned for a visit, he took us down to his wine cellar. He showed us where he kept his ordinary wines and then showed us a cupboard where his special wines were kept. He said, "I only use these when very special old friends visit." There was a pause and then he said, "I guess this is such an occasion." We enjoyed the wine.

We spent one Christmas day with the Schulzes. They were all musical. Jim joined their musical group, and we spent the afternoon singing and listening to German and American carols.

Madame Gazaigne was the wife of the commandant of the French Garrison in Karlsruhe. She had been educated at Heidelberg University and spoke fluent German. Since she didn't speak English and I couldn't speak French, we communicated in German. She and Major Gazaigne had three sons. Jacque, their middle son, became a good friend to Jim. He enjoyed running Jim's electric trains and came over often to visit. I still keep in touch with Jacque, now chief urologist at a large hospital in Bourges.

Madame Gazaigne and I took turns preparing meals and hosting both families. Her meals were more complicated than mine. They consisted of several courses – each with a different wine and served on a new plate. Years later, when I visited her in France, after such a fancy meal, I ended up spending an entire afternoon washing dishes. Her son had been injured while riding his moped. He had been taking exams to enter the university, and the accident had caused him to miss a session. Without proper papers from the hospital, school, and some government agency showing he had been injured, he would have had to wait a year to repeat the exam. Chuck, Madame Gazaigne, and her son spent the afternoon getting all the necessary forms. I was glad I wasn't a French housewife.

Christmas And Other Recollections

While we were in Karlsruhe, we needed someone to help with Mary. We asked around and were able to hire a student from West Technical University. Henrietta Kaspersmeir was majoring in home economics and physical education. She was from Erkeln in Northern Germany. Both of her parents were teachers in a small school, and they lived in an apartment near the school.

The first Christmas we were in Germany, they invited us to their home. We spent a few days with Henny's folks in Erkeln and then went to Fulda, which was near the East German border. I remember seeing the wall. We stayed in a guesthouse and in the evening decided to climb up the hill to a small Benedictine chapel for Christmas Eve services. It had been snowing, and the whole city was like a magical scene.

The chapel was lit with candles. The Holy Family was wrapped in cloth, which would be removed at midnight. Cyclamen in various shades were blooming in front of the masked figures. We sang hymns and then at the stroke of midnight the wraps were removed and Mary, Joseph, and Jesus appeared before us. We sang "Stille Nacht, Heilige Nacht" in hushed voices. I felt tears streaming down my face. Memories of my childhood appeared. I was homesick.

I wished my parents could have been there, but they were far away. We left the chapel, and as we walked down the hill, I thought of the hymn "O Little Town of Bethlehem"!

True, there was snow – not desert – but the town below looked so beautiful bathed in white with twinkling lights. After Fulda, we traveled to Nuremburg, Munich, and Vienna.

Another Christmas, we went to Henny's and stayed in Brakel in a guesthouse. The family had moved by then. The lights in the town square were all white, not colored as we had had in the States. In the morning, we received bags of nuts and candy before going to Henny's home. We had a white wine and tapioca soup for the appetizer and goose for the entree with a pudding for dessert. Years later I mentioned to Renata (Henny's sister) about having our first taste of goose, and she remarked that her mother had only prepared goose that one time especially for us as they usually ate sauerbraten.

In the late afternoon of Christmas Day, we were invited to come into the living room by the ringing of a bell. The doors to the room had been kept closed up to that time. As we entered, there was a tree on a revolving stand playing a beautiful Christmas carol. The tree was lit with real candles that twinkled in the dim light of the room. There was a long table covered with gifts and colorfully decorated paper plates holding candy, cookies, and nuts. We enjoyed our gifts and then had afternoon coffee and Kuchen.

The 26th of December is known in Germany as the second Christmas Day. This is the day family and friends visit each other. One person we got to know was Helmut, who later married Renata.

I can't recall how many days we stayed with Henny's family, but I do recall that on our way home, we always had to stop at the Army snack bar near the place where General Patton was injured to eat a turkey dinner. If we hadn't eaten turkey on Christmas Day, Chuck would have felt he hadn't had a proper Christmas dinner.

Jim became fluent in German. Herr Kaspersmeir remarked one morning at breakfast that Jim had awakened during the night and asked, "Wo bin ich?" (Where am I?). Chuck and I began to speak and understand the language too. We had taken a few lessons in Karlsruhe, and I had worked with Frau Pils. People used to say Chuck had perfect grammar, but I sounded more like a German. Sometimes people would ask whether I was a German war bride or whether my folks had come from Germany.

During our five years in Germany, I think we spent most Christmases in northern Germany with Henny's family. We took many walks, as Germans especially enjoy afternoon walks. We were informed that it was obvious we didn't walk often because we tended to walk quickly. Those who do walk often walk slowly. We also explored the nearby countryside by car. We visited many cathedrals and monasteries as well as museums, castles, and other historic areas. I found the old German villages and cities each held a treasure of things to see and experience.

The Kaspersmeirs also visited us in Karlsruhe. Henny met Zia, who was a Moslem from Turkey, at the International Student Center in Karlsruhe. While her parents were visiting us, they also met Zia. Since Henny's family was Catholic, they vehemently opposed Henny's dating Zia. As the romance progressed, Frau Kaspersmeir became more and more upset with Henny. I think she threatened to disinherit her if she continued to date Zia. Nevertheless the romance continued, and Henny eventually married Zia in Karlsruhe and moved to Izmir, Turkey, where Zia practices as an architect. During Frau Kaspersmeir's lifetime, she never visited Zia and Henny in Turkey, and I don't think Zia ever was welcome in her home. We tried in vain to tell Henny's family they'd lose their daughter if they didn't accept her husband. After the mother's death, her husband did visit Turkey, and today after his death, Renata and Helmut either visit in Turkey or Henny and Zia go to Germany.

The Askews - British Friends And Family

Sometime during our first year in Europe, we decided to take a trip to England, the home of my ancestors. We took Jim and went to London. It was so wonderful for me to hear English being spoken all around us. One afternoon, we went to Saint James Park. Chuck went to an outdoor cafe to get us tea and cake. While there, he saw a man with a boy of Jim's age. Chuck suggested that the boy get his mother and take her to the table where I was sitting while his father got the food. The boy obeyed and so began our acquaintance with the Askews.

Dick was a teacher, Pat was a homemaker, and Richard was their son. The Askews invited us to visit them at their home in Colchester, which we did on another trip. I remember Pat telling me she thought I was extravagant because Jim had no mended clothes while Richard's play pants had mended knees.

We visited their family several times while we lived in Europe. They showed us Saxon ruins, Roman ruins, old villages, and historic cities. We witnessed Britain through the eyes of a Brit.

One year, we invited them to come to Germany and from there, accompany us to Italy. We had a blue Chevrolet, which Richard thought was really something special as it was bigger than their car. He would lean out of the window and put up his thumb to show everyone how great life was.

When we reached the Alps, there was snow on the ground. Richard shouted, "Let me out." We stopped the car, and the boys had a snowball fight. It was the first time Richard had ever seen snow. We spent the first night in a Tyrolean inn in the Dolomites. This region was part of Italy, but the locals spoke German since it had been part of Austria before the First World War. It was just before Easter, and the shepherds had come down from the mountains. They had spent the day drinking at the inn and were really far gone. One shepherd had his head on the table. He raised it slightly and said, "If I go home, this party will break up." One of the other shepherds asked me to dance and became quite persistent when I declined. I was saved by the proprietor who told him there was to be no dancing until after Easter. One of the shepherds told me he could speak English. "What can you say?" I asked. His reply was, "I love you, my darling." I wonder if he really understood what he said. I decided not to pursue it. From there, we continued on to Venice where we had a gondola ride and enjoyed seeing the city.

On one trip to England, we were invited to go to the shore for the day. It was a cloudy day with the temperature in the low seventies. In the States, I would never have chosen this day to swim. My British friends thought it was a lovely day, since Britain has so much rain. From their perspective, it was a beautiful day. They enjoyed a swim, but I declined.

I have kept up with the Askews over the years. Both Dick and Pat have died. Richard attended Oxford and became a barrister. He works for an insurance company and investigates claims worldwide. He told us about one incident involving Chinese pirates who had hijacked a British ship off the coast of China. The pirates took the ship up the China coast and changed the smokestack to make the ship appear different. I can't recall what cargo the ship was carrying, but as a result of this, electronic chips were put in future cargoes so that they could be traced.

While we lived in Europe, I decided to look up my British family. I knew a distant cousin, Gordon Perkins, lived near Bath. When my Aunt Ada was alive, he would visit her. He had served on some of the British ships that came into New York. I remember one winter day when he walked to Englewood from the George Washington Bridge. How he knew the way, I never did discover.

I found Gordon's address and contacted him. We were invited to visit him and his wife, Madeline, at their home near Bradford-on-Avon. Through Gordon, I got to meet other family members and learned a bit about our family history. Gordon's grandmother and my great grandmother were sisters.

Tina, left, and Emma, who were employed as maids for the Latimers for 19 years in Panama

Our Domestic Help

Our first maid was Erna. We hired her to help with our housework and help with Mary when Henny was not available. Erna had been married and had had two children, a boy and a girl. Her husband was called to serve in the German army and he never returned from the Russian front. The two children died from a disease for which they had not been vaccinated, probably diphtheria. In order to get food and shelter, before coming to us, she had lived with a black American soldier. With him, she had a son who was mentally handicapped, and at that time was in a children's home. I don't think she ever saw him. At first, I felt like condemning her for living with someone out of wedlock, but as I thought more about it, I wondered whether I might not have done the same in order to survive.

Erna lived with us several months until one day when I couldn't find Mary. I asked Erna where she was. She couldn't seem to remember where she had taken her. We searched and found her outside our apartment. I felt Erna was no longer capable of caring for Mary and had to go. When we cleaned her room, we found it lined with clean bottles and jars. There was room for only her bed. It seems she thought she'd need them for making jam or juice sometime.

Our second maid, part time, was Lori. She had had training to become a servant and was an excellent worker. She was married to Hans, and both of them loved Mary. Lori had no children of her own. When we took trips, Lori and Hans would stay in our home and care for Mary. We had by this time moved from our apartment on base to a duplex we shared with the Brown family. Lori continued to work for us until we left Germany. We kept in touch for many years because she enjoyed hearing about Mary and her progress.

Natasha

Sometimes, a good secretary is hard to find. This was the case in the Dependents Education Group until Natasha came along. Natasha was from Leningrad, Russia. Her parents had been professors at the university. During the siege of St. Petersburg during World War II, the Russians laid tracks over the ice on the lake to be able to evacuate civilians from the city. Natasha and her parents were among the lucky ones to escape. The escape route let to Stalingrad. Along the way, Natasha's father died, and his body was thrown off the train.

Natasha and her mother were captured by the German troops. Since they both spoke German, Frau Malchevsky was put to work in a hospital, and Natasha became a secretary. When the Germans retreated, Natasha and her mother went with them. To do otherwise would have meant their deaths. They travelled through the Ukraine, Romania, and Hungary before reaching Germany (Bavaria).

Eventually, the two women came to Karlsruhe where Frau Malchevsky was hired as a professor at the university, and Natasha became a secretary for the American military. Just before coming to Karlsruhe, she married a German journalist and bore one child, Vera. By the time I knew her, she was divorced from her husband and lived with her mother and daughter.

Natasha spoke and wrote perfect English. Some of the American officers did not write well, and Natasha would correct their work. This did not please the officers, so they didn't want her to work for them. When Chuck heard she was available, he immediately asked to have her work for him. She was not a threat to him. They worked perfectly together.

After about two years, Natasha became ill with cancer. She worked until she was too weak to sit at her desk. Sometimes, there were foods she'd crave which weren't available on the German market. If I could get them through the military, I would buy them and take them to her. She tried many different treatments, but none worked, and she died after about one year.

We kept up with Frau Malchevsky and Vera for several years after Natasha's death. Frau Malchevsky's brother, a scientist, had been banished to Siberia. Sometime after Natasha's death, he contacted his sister to say he had been released and would be travelling to Leningrad. He wanted her to meet him there. Frau Malchevsky and Vera did go there. The three of them went to their former home, dug up the family silver, which they had buried in the back yard, and carried it back to Germany. I don't know who had been living in the house after they left.

Memories Of Trips

One of the last trips we took while living in Europe was a drive to France and Italy. We then took a ferry to Greece and drove back to Germany through Yugoslavia. In all, we drove 5000 miles. It was springtime. We passed through an Italian village on Easter Sunday, and I recall in one village seeing men carrying huge crosses on their backs and wearing crowns of thorns on their heads as penance. The men looked exhausted.

We took a ship from Brindisi in Italy to Corfu, a Greek island. There, we witnessed a second Easter as the Greek Orthodox Church celebrates Easter at a different time than the Roman Catholic Church. There were processions of

Atilla and Rita Yakara, a couple the Latimers sponsored to become American citizens

church officials down the main street of the island. Women placed their babies on the street where the procession would pass. When the officials reached the babies, they would stop and bless them. The women knew their babies wouldn't be trampled on or hurt.

As we journeyed on through Greece, we saw many red blankets on the ground where they had been placed to dry. Apparently, the custom required washing bedding in the spring. When we stopped to have a picnic, local villagers gathered, hoping we would share our food. Among them was an old shepherdess who spoke some German. In the towns, we witnessed pascal lambs being prepared for Easter. The skins were removed by putting a bicycle pump under the skin near the dead animal's foot and pumping air into the area. The skin blew up like a balloon and could be easily removed. Later, we saw lambs on spits outside homes with children turning the spits over a charcoal fire. What a delicious smell!

We traveled over one road where we saw no cars for hours. Suddenly, a bus appeared, barreling down the road. The bus hit the side of our car and never stopped. Luckily we weren't hurt, and the car could still be driven.

While we were in Greece, we visited Delphi. It was the time of the Easter vacation, and all the Greeks who lived in Athens had come home for the holiday. All the hotels were full in Delphi. We asked where we might find a place to stay and were told there might be a place in Agrinion. By this time, it was getting near evening. We started out, but got behind a huge trailer carrying a large piece of machinery. The road was narrow, and we crept along. When we finally reached the hotel, we found they had rooms, but they were primitive. The bed sheets were coarse, like canvas used for sails. There were donkeys in the room on the other side of the wall. We had no choice but to stay. When we complained that there were no lights in the community bath, the lady said, in French, "Il est malade," meaning "it is sick." We went to the kitchen to point out what we wanted to eat for dinner. Evidently, we didn't point well because we were very sick the next day.

In the following days, we visited ruins in Athens, Sparta, and Mycenae. We stopped at Meteora (a monastery on a mountain). In the past, monks used baskets and ropes to get to the top since the cliffs were vertical. By the time we got there, an elevator had been built. There were nuns present who wanted to touch Jim, as they saw few children. Jim was not at all happy to be fondled by strangers.

We continued on to Yugoslavia and spent the night at Skopja. We stopped at a first class hotel, but they wanted to double the price of the room. We had a hotel guide that listed the room prices. A British couple also argued about the room prices, but the person on the desk wouldn't back down. We left and went to another hotel, which had a lower rating. We ordered dinner off the menu and waited. After maybe 10 minutes, the waiter returned and said they didn't have what we had ordered. We tried again with the same result. We finally asked what they did have and were told lamb. We finally got a lamb dinner.

As we waited for dinner, all the lights went out, and we were completely in the dark. There was a huge picture of Tito, the dictator of Yugoslavia, on the wall near us. As we sat there in the dark, we wondered whether one of us might disappear or something sinister might happen before the lights came on. Fortunately, nothing happened.

An English Adventure

On one trip to England, we were in a small village at lunchtime. Our custom was to have a picnic by the side of the road or in a park. Chuck parked the car, and I set out to get food. In those days, there were no supermarkets. I went to the butcher to get meat, the bakery for bread, the green grocer for fruit and vegetables, and the dairy for milk. I think it was on this trip that our niece Carol was with us.

The dairy was in part of a house. When I entered, there was a counter and a bell. I rang the bell, and the door behind the counter opened. A lady wearing an apron came out and asked what I wanted. I told her I wanted milk. She said it wasn't possible to give me any. I had seen a truck with bottles of milk in front of the house. These bottles were to be delivered to clients. I needed a carton, but the bus bringing clips to close these cartons hadn't come, and she had no way to close the cartons. I suggested a pin, which she agreed might work. In the end, she managed to close one with the pin, and I got my milk. When I returned to the car, Chuck said, "Where in the world have you been? I thought you were lost." Jim and Carol, our niece from North Carolina, were more than anxious for my return. I explained that this village didn't have the facilities we had, and I felt sorry for the women of the town who must spend so much time shopping.

Paris Trips

Chuck always had a conference in Paris in early November. We would stay in a small family hotel on Rue Pergolese, the Hotel Sylva. There was a bakery nearby where we could get croissants filled with chocolate. How good they tasted! We at first locked our car, which we parked on the street. One night, the side front window was broken. After that, we kept the car unlocked and put a cigarette in the glove compartment. Each morning the cigarette was gone.

While Chuck attended his meetings, Jim and I explored Paris. Jim turned out to be an excellent guide although he was only 10. We especially enjoyed Napoleon's tomb and puppet shows.

Other Trips We Took

Fortunately, to help my memory, we wrote Christmas letters each year, and I have all of them, dating back to 1948. Memories, I find, fade, and one forgets what year things happened. Looking back, I discovered we attended the Brussels World's Fair in 1958. In the spring, we enjoyed Holland, and we went to Italy in July. In 1959, Chuck served his naval reserve duty on the aircraft carrier "Forrestal" in the Mediterranean. Jim and I took the train to Naples, leaving Karlsruhe at 2:30 a.m. After we met Chuck, we traveled back home through Italy. We attended a Christmas Mass at St. Peter's and visited Florence with its many museums. On the train, passengers shared their panatoni bread with us. I think of Italy each Christmas when I see this type of bread in the market.

Mother's Illness And Death

In the summer of 1959, we took leave to visit the States. When we arrived in New Jersey, we found my mother very ill. I knew something was wrong when I saw a dirty bathroom. She was in pain, and Dr. Phillips had put her in the hospital. In those days, not much medication was given, and mother was in agony. I was to set to sail back home on the S.S. Constitution the week after mother entered the hospital. When I talked with the doctor, he said I'd better stay, as mother had terminal cancer, and it was in the last stage. Jim and Chuck went back as planned, but Mary and I stayed with Dad. Mother lived about a week more and died on October 29.

After the funeral, I stayed to help Dad get rid of Mother's clothes and straighten out their apartment. During this time, I got to see a lot of Dad's sister, Pearle, and her friend Florence. I had hoped to be back by Thanksgiving, but one morning, I got a call from Aunt Florence saying that Aunt Pearle was unresponsive. She had had a massive stroke. I decided to stay on to see if she would recover, but she never did. She was put in the county hospital and died in February of the following year. I had lost two people whom I truly loved. Mary and I returned to Germany by plane in early December.

Dad's Visit

After Mother's death, Dad decided to visit us in Europe. He came in May on the S.S. Constitution. We met him in Munich and took him with us to see the passion play in Oberammergau. We sat outdoors wrapped in blankets for four hours in the morning and the afternoon. We were so cold at lunch, we had tea with rum to warm us.

When July came, Dad wanted to visit the area near Verdun where he had fought in World War I. We decided to take him on our way to London where Chuck had naval reserve duty. He got as far as Sainte Menehould when the left front tie rod of the car snapped. We were on a hill and just managed to steer the car to the side of the road. The front wheels looked like they were pigeon-toed. Neighbors came out of their homes to look and then promptly went back in and closed the blinds. Chuck walked to a French police station and put in a call to the American headquarters in Verdun for help. At first, it was indicated no help could be sent because there hadn't been an accident. After Chuck explained that there would be one, it was agreed a wrecker would be sent. We waited and waited. Finally, we took Dad to the station, which was nearby, to take a train to London.

After a wrecker had not arrived in over an hour, Chuck

returned to the police station and put in another call. The wrecker had gone to another town 80 miles away. About this time, an American salesman stopped by and asked if we needed help. We said we did, and he agreed to take Jim and me to Verdun to get a room for the night.

We waited there for Chuck who finally arrived at about 3 a.m. The next day, we hired some GIs who found a wrecked police car, which had the tie rod we needed. We left as soon as the car was fixed and drove to the French port to catch the ship for England. We arrived in London the next morning, and Chuck reported to duty on time. When the admiral heard our story, he told Chuck to take the day off, and we went to find Dad, who couldn't believe we had really gotten to London on time.

Summer And Fall 1961

We returned to New Jersey to visit Dad in the summer of 1961. We had been with him only a few days when Mary became very ill with vomiting and diarrhea. I couldn't get her to drink enough fluids. I got up in the night to check on her and got little response. I was afraid she was dying. We rushed her to the hospital where they told me her veins had collapsed from dehydration. She was put on the danger list. Chuck or I had to be with her at all times. A woman doctor saw her when she was admitted but in the morning a male doctor visited. Imagine my surprise when I realized it was the doctor who had cared for me when I had polio. He took wonderful care of Mary. A tube was placed in her foot and she received fluids. Before this illness, Mary had often appeared to really not care whether she lived or died. Afterwards, she had a different attitude. She never admitted to being ill, and in fact hardly ever is.

It was during this vacation that we learned Dad had leukemia. He needed blood transfusions and was put on prednisone. We got a woman to come daily to help him after we left.

We returned to Germany by plane via Gander, Newfoundland, and Shannon, Ireland. In the fall, we sent Jim to the Goethe Gymnasium so he could learn German.

A Christmas Letter Chuck Wrote
For 1962

In the beginning of October, Chuck attended a conference sponsored by the French Ministry of Education at the Sevres Centre International Pedagogique. In November, he goes to Italy for a teachers' conference and a visit to each of the schools there. He is scheduled during January to fly to the United States to interview teacher candidates for the system for the coming year. While there, he will probably also be looking for a job himself, as we definitely have decided to return home this year. We thought about returning last year, but the right opportunity never seemed to present itself. At any rate, you can plan on next year's letter coming from a different location. (Maybe from two locations if Chuck gets called up to active naval duty).

Alice has been helping out again this fall teaching in the Army enlisted education program - teaching English and history to soldiers who have not completed elementary school.

We sent Jimmy to the Goethe Gymnasium in the fall of 1961. His ability was such that he was about 2 1/2 years above norm in our schools, and we were considering moving him to the next grade, but decided that a year in a host-nation school would provide even more of a challenge. He went to the middle of grade 5 in the German school (he had begun grade

4 in our school) and had plenty to do learning new concepts as well as the German language. His handwriting and spelling (even in English) improved greatly, and he enjoyed the experience. He liked "turnen" (physical education with emphasis upon gymnastics) best. He rode his bike back and forth to school, had about four hours daily in school, six days a week. At the beginning of November, he had a week's vacation, but he was tutored a couple hours daily by our friend, Henny Kaspersmeir (who used to live with us and now taught in Schwetzingen near Heidelberg).

Mary goes to nursery school two days per week. Her vocabulary has increased greatly, but she is not yet ready for kindergarten. She is a very happy child and a joy to have around.

This has not been a very relaxed fall in Europe, as I am sure you all realize. However, one cannot stay in a state of tension forever so one becomes numb to it all. We face each day with a prayer that path can be trod through the maze that will bring us all out into the sunshine eventually, but the danger is ever around us. Preparedness and firmness is our watchword. Never in our history have we as a nation had more in material sense, but probably never have we faced a more uncertain future. This Christmas will certainly be a time when we will need to renew our Christian strength.

May the Christmas spirit be in the hearts of all of you in the far corners of the earth. We wish we could write to each of you individually. We appreciate the letters we get and hope you will send them again this year.

Alice, Chuck, Jimmy, and Mary Latimer

This was the time of the Berlin crisis. In a letter Chuck wrote at Christmas, which is printed above, he expressed his feelings about the event. It was during this year that we began to think about returning to the States. We felt we should be closer to Dad, and we also felt if Chuck were to be able to get a position in the States, we shouldn't be many years overseas. Both Teachers College and Harvard interviewed Chuck and thought he should apply to a school system where he would become a superintendent. A community in the Lake Minetonka District of Minnesota offered him a position. He was about to accept when the placement office at Teachers College asked him to interview for a position as dean of a junior college in the Panama Canal Zone. Chuck said he didn't want to go overseas again, but he was persuaded to interview. Chuck was offered a trip down to Panama to see the area, and he decided to go. When he heard we could have a maid and that I could teach, he decided to accept the position. It certainly beat the long cold winters of Minnesota when I would have been housebound with Mary.

The children and I left for Bremerhaven by train. Once there, we boarded a troop ship, the USS Buchner. Our accommodations did not equal the "America." Off Nantucket, we got into fog and the foghorn blew night and day for two days. A neighbor in Upper Montclair had gone down when the "Andrea Doria" sank. I couldn't help but think of that.

When we arrived in New York, we were met by Dad's friend Chester Bogert. He said Dad was dying and was in the hospital. I wondered why my visits home seemed to occur when someone I loved was dying.

I spent a week going between the hospital and Dad's apartment. Jim stayed with Mary, although he was only 10. One day, I had to go to Montclair because the movers had to get furniture from the attic of our old home. I stopped at the hospital to check on Dad and found he had just died. That was June 28, 1962. We had Dad's funeral a couple of days later. My cousins, the Maugers and Jim Clitter, came.

Our Volkswagen arrived at Port Newark right after the funeral. I went to get the car. I no longer remember how I got to Newark. When I went to check the car out, I was missing one paper, and the authorities didn't want to give me the car. After much pleading, I was finally given the keys.

Right after Dad's death, I knew I had to get the children to Chuck's parents in Charleston. I got tickets for them through a travel agent. The day I was to take them to the airport, American Airlines went on strike. When I got to the airport, the agent informed me there were no seats for the children despite their having reservations. I was so tired, upset, and angry that I began to sob. Jim began to tell the agent he was to blame for my crying. All the people in line said, "Can't you see the woman needs help? Get these children seats." They reached Charleston safely.

I now had the task of cleaning out Dad's apartment. One day the phone rang. The call was from Rita and Atilla Yakar who were in New York. We had agreed to sponsor them to come to the States. They had arrived at just the right time. I gave them many of Dad's things and paid a month's rent on his apartment. Chester took them to buy a car, and Atilla got his driver's license and a job with Sears Roebuck.

We were free to go to Panama. Chuck had by this time arrived from Germany. We headed first to Charleston to get the children, then to New Orleans to get on the Panama Canal ship "Christobal." I drove Dad's Oldsmobile, and Chuck drove the VW. Jim got pneumonia along the way, but a stop in Atlanta at my cousin Virginia's home and a visit to the doctor for a penicillin shot enabled him to recover rather quickly. We made it safely to the ship and enjoyed our four-day trip as well as meeting new friends.

Panama, We Are Here

Our first home was a duplex. The first night I started to cook dinner, I heated the oven, and cockroaches –maybe 15 of them—poured out. I'm sure my neighbors heard my screams.

We adjusted quickly. I began teaching, and Chuck took over the administration of the college. We started out with two Indian maids, but they began quarreling one morning over which one would pour our orange juice. The younger of the two had a baby, "Americus," who cried all Christmas Day. I thought we had baby Jesus in our maid's room. We later got two other maids, Emma and Tina, who stayed with us 19 years. I didn't mention that Mary caught pneumonia from Jim, and she was ill for three weeks. Fortunately, we had met a pediatrician, Dr. Byron Efthimiadis, on the ship, and he cared for Mary; later he and his family became good friends of ours.

Soon after we arrived, we were invited to go on an LST (Landing Ship Tanker) to Portobello to see the "Festival of the Black Christ." There was no road at that time going to this town, and one had to go by ship. We spent the late morning and afternoon there. By the end of the day, the town was noisy with many drunken people. We were told we needed to quickly get on the LST to go back to Panama City. We thought the haste was because the authorities were concerned about our safety. We found out later the Navy had been put on alert because of the Bay of Pigs conflict.

My Teaching Career

My first teaching job in the Canal Zone was at Diablo Junior High. I was assigned to classrooms, which were about a block apart. In one, I taught Home Economics. I had 20 students but only eight sewing machines. Because of the humidity (90 percent), the machines would get rusty and wouldn't work. The girls would get impatient because they couldn't use the machines. I had to learn machine repair in a hurry.

In addition to sewing, I taught cooking. When food

Alice teaching a home economics class in the Canal Zone

was still in the oven, I couldn't leave the room, which meant my English class would be nearly out of control when I got there. The home economic classes were taught in the morning, and I had English classes to teach in the afternoon. The class was taught in a wooden building with a tin roof. At first, we had no air conditioning.

I'd start the class, and suddenly someone would shout, "Mrs. Latimer, Maria is falling!" Maria had seizures and would fall out of her chair and land on the floor. I'd try to reach her before she landed.

The students hated English and would think of all sorts of ways to disrupt the class. One boy, Danny, liked to pretend his desk was a drum. To make matters worse, the rain started at about 2 p.m. It was a torrential tropical rain that pounded on the roof and made it impossible for me to be heard. We would stop and the students would read or do written work. I often wonder how much I really taught them.

Balboa High School

After a year at Diablo Junior High, I was asked to teach Home Economics at Balboa High School. There, I taught not only cooking and sewing, but also home decoration and child care. I had 18-20 girls per class. While we worked on cooking, the girls gave a tea for their mothers, which gave me a chance to meet more of the Canal Zone women.

One afternoon, I received a call from an upset mother who told me her daughter's boyfriend was going to meet her after school, and they planned to go to Panama to get married. The parents didn't dislike the boy; they just didn't want their daughter to get married two weeks before graduation. I was asked to intervene. I found the girl in the restroom changing into a better dress. She said she was going to be married that afternoon. I asked her to get her boyfriend and bring him to my room. She did, and we discussed the pros and cons of the present situation. After school, I accompanied the couple to the girl's home for a discussion with her parents. In the end, they waited and after graduation had a church wedding. Some years later, I met them at a reunion, and they were the happy parents of four children.

In January of 1964, in response to concerns over sovereignty, Governor Fleming decided that the American flag would not be flown in front of Balboa High School. On the seventh, a group of five Canal College students raised the American flag. An hour later, the flag was taken down by Mr. Speir, the high school principal. After another half hour passed, the students, encouraged by some parents, again raised a flag, but this time, it was a smaller one. This one was allowed to stay.

Meanwhile, in Panama, there had been rumors of a strike. The flag incident gave people in Panama a chance to strike out at the Americans. By afternoon, people from Panama began coming into the zone. They threw over trash cans and stole clothes that were hanging under the houses or any other items they could lay their hands on.

I was at school, but I left quickly and took the back road to get home. I could hear the noise of the crowd. By evening, the crowd had become violent and was throwing Molotov Cocktails. They had been given large quantities of rum. Our house was located high on the hill with a commanding view of Panama City. We went out and stood on the edge of the hill near our house. We could see the fires below. Shortly after dusk, as we were starting dinner, helicopters with loud speakers announced that the Canal Zone was under martial law by order of General Andrew O'Meara.

By midnight, we had a personnel carrier with soldiers carrying submachine guns under our house. We could hear bullets being fired in our direction. I didn't go to school for three days. When I attempted to leave the house, a policeman usually told me to go back inside to avoid being shot.

After our soldiers took charge and the violence slowed down, we returned to our jobs. However, it wasn't safe to drive a car with Canal Zone license plates into Panama. We attended a wedding at the Union Club, but we were taken there in a car with Panamanian plates. Life didn't really return to normal for six months.

Being A Guidance Counselor

After seven years teaching home economics, my back began to give me trouble. Standing to teach gave me back pain. There was an opening in the guidance department, and I was asked whether I'd like to change jobs. I had no official training in counseling, but I had often found that students came to me with their problems, and I enjoyed working with them. I got the job with the understanding I'd go to Penn State University for two summers and get a master's degree. At that time, Penn State had professors in Panama giving courses there. We also had student teachers in our schools.

I continued in the counseling department until my retirement in 1981. During my time in the counseling office, I had some unusual duties. One day, I was told an iguana was walking down the hall trying to get into some of the classrooms. I called for the janitor to come and "rescue" the creature, but he would have nothing to do with it. I left my office to look for the iguana. I spotted it again, trying to get into a classroom. Fortunately, it wasn't so large that it was dangerous. A large one uses its tail for defense and can cut a person to the bone. I picked it up by the tail and carried it to the biology lab. They had a crate to keep it in until a student could take it home.

One morning, I had a call from a mother who explained her son had a large snake (nonpoisonous), which he kept in a cage at the foot of the stairs leading to their apartment. Her husband had been in the hospital after a heart attack. He hated snakes, and she was afraid when he came home he might have another heart attack. She had asked Bob to remove the snake, but he had paid no attention to her. She wondered if I could get the snake removed. Fortunately I knew Bob well, as he had been in my office several times. I went to his classroom and asked whether he could guess why his mother had called me. He knew, but said his father was foolish to be afraid of snakes. I convinced him it would be better not to take a chance that something might happen. Together we went to his home. He said he had a large bag we could put the snake in, and he knew a man who would be glad to have the snake.

On the way to the house, I told Bob he needed to be sure he had a rope around the bag that was tightly wrapped because I really didn't like snakes, and I didn't want to drive off the road if the snake came near me. When we got to the house, I saw a snake about five feet long. I held the bag while Bob used a forked stick to hold its head down. He picked the snake up by the tail, and together we got it into the car. We delivered it safely to Bob's friend. Forever after, I had a grateful mother on my side.

Jim's High School Years

I sometimes think it was hard for Jim to have his mother teaching at the school he was attending. He wasn't able to get his driver's license until his senior year because of his age. He went to school each day with me and repeatedly told me he wished he could drive.

He gave us a scare early in his junior year when he went camping in the jungle with the Scouts along the Los Cruces Trail. He left the group on a Saturday night, and no one knew where he was when the Scouts reached the end of the trail on Sunday. We had helicopters out looking for him and were told troops would scour the jungle later if he hadn't been found. On Sunday, there were prayer services held at churches, and people gathered at our house. Fortunately, he walked out unharmed, except for a black palm needle that had to be removed. He never really understood why we were upset. He had followed streams and had eaten peanut butter he had carried with him.

Jim was selected to attend National Science Foundation workshops at both the University of North Carolina and the Colorado School of Mines. He was active in the Junior ROTC during his high school years. During his senior year, he served as Battalion Executive Officer. In addition to his ROTC work and scouting, he was the concertmaster for his high school orchestra, he played violin in a quartet, and acted in plays. Chuck and I were busy trying to keep up with all of his activities. He was selected to attend Rice University under the early decision plan. After he left for college, our house seemed quiet, and we couldn't wait for him to return at Christmas. He had hoped to get into the Naval ROTC at Rice, but high blood pressure prevented him from doing so. We later learned that the decongestants he had been taking for allergies caused the high blood pressure.

Anastasio

Our gardener was a tiny Indian. He used a machete to loosen the dirt when he needed to work with the heavy soil. All one had to do to get a plant growing was to cut off a stalk and stick it into the ground. We had orchids, anthurium, and red ginger around the house.

One day, the gardener came with a clipping from a funeral home showing a coffin. He said his son had died, and he needed money to bury him. Anastasio liked his liquor, and knowing this, Chuck gave him a check made out to the funeral home. We went to church the next day and mentioned this to friends who also hired Anastasio. They laughed and said he had buried many sons with the use of the clipping. The check came back signed with an X. Anastasio had gotten his alcohol.

Wildlife

Our house was situated close to the governor's home with jungle above and below us. Marmosets lived in the part above us. Each morning, one or more would jump across the road from a tree on one side to a tree on the other. From the tree, they would go to our clothesline and then to the railing leading to our kitchen window. Once there, they would chatter until one of us opened the door and gave them a piece of banana. They held the banana in their two front feet while their back feet held the railing and their tails went straight down to keep their balance. After finishing the banana they would lick each finger clean.

Another animal we continued to see was an iguana. We had one about five-six feet long that was often seen in the kapok tree outside our living room window. One time, he was on the ground in front of our house. Elena's son-in-law was at the house and got too near the old creature. The iguana lashed his tale at Carlos, who fortunately managed to jump out of the way. If Carlos had been hit by the tail, he probably would have been cut to the bone. The tail acts like a razor.

Another animal we saw frequently was the coatimundi. They look a bit like raccoons, except they are bigger and have long tails. When they walk through talk grass, their tails are straight up in the air. When a group of them move about, all one sees is a series of tall tails in the grass.

A friend told me she had looked out of her kitchen window one morning, and there, just outside, was a deer with a coatimundi on its back, apparently scratching its back. The deer had learned how to get a massage.

One morning, I went to our kitchen and there was a white-faced monkey. He had opened the back door and gotten in. Before I could get a banana to coax him out, he went down the hall to Jim's bedroom. He jumped on one of the twin beds, and then, jumped to the other. He leaped up on the dresser and spent time looking at himself in the mirror. By that time, I had gotten a banana, which I offered to him. He followed me back to the kitchen and out the back door. We never found out whether he was someone's pet who had escaped or just where he had come from. I knew no one at school would believe me if I said I was late because of a monkey.

Seeing Gold

Shortly after arriving in Panama, we were invited to the home of a woman doctor. She had a male friend who was also invited. After dinner, she asked if we'd be interested in looking at some pre-Colombian gold pieces. We agreed we would. She asked her friend to get the gold to show us. He went to his car, opened the trunk, and took out a pillowcase full of 24 karat gold pieces (huacas) taken from Indian graves found on the Azuero Peninsula. There were bracelets, breastplates, headpieces, and many other types of adornment. The pieces covered the dining room table. I was astonished. He offered to sell me a large gold piece, which could be used as a necklace for $1700.00. I declined. I couldn't imagine walking around with that much gold. While we were in Bogota, Columbia, we visited the gold museum. We were taken into a huge vault and saw pieces such as we had seen that night in Panama. However, the collection was much larger.

At one of the Canal Zone College Club meetings, a jeweler came with his four-year-old daughter. She had on the gold filigree jewelry, which is typically worn with the pollera. There are pieces for the hair as well as those to be worn around the neck or as pins. Most pieces have a precious stone set in them (diamond, pearl, ruby, or sapphire). The young girl was wearing each type of piece. We asked how much the entire collection was worth and the jeweler said about $85,000.00. I'd be afraid of being robbed if I ever had that much jewelry.

Social Events

We made many friends while we were in Panama. They included the family of the doctor who had cared for Mary. Through knowing him and his family, we were invited to many parties held by the Panamanian Greek community. I especially enjoyed going to the Raymundos. They had a penthouse overlooking the city. After a huge dinner, we enjoyed Greek dances on the roof. Dr. Efthimiadis has since died, and his daughter has become a pediatrician.

When Chuck later became deputy school superintendent, we entertained almost monthly at our home. Every official who came from Washington was given a cocktail party. Jim would often play the piano for the guests since he can play by ear as well as read music; he was quite a hit. Sometimes, he'd play for over an hour. Our maids weren't too happy with all the entertaining. They complained we ran a hotel.

We had access to the officers clubs and had many wonderful parties there. The club at Fort Amador was right by the ocean, and the view was spectacular. When we were first there, the old Tivoli Guest House, where President Teddy Roosevelt had entertained, was standing. The old building, which was wooden, was eventually torn down. While it stood, we enjoyed going there and imagining what entertainment must have been like in the early 1900s.

A couple who entertained at the clubs were the Marshalls, John and Mary Ann. Mary Ann was blind, but she was a great pianist. John played bass. One time they were at our house, and we were showing slides. I asked if everyone could see the screen, and Mary Ann said, "I can't." She had a wonderful sense of humor. John was her eyes.

Another time, in our church, the Balboa Union Church, it was Easter, and I was wearing red patent leather pumps. John said to Mary Ann, "You should see Alice's red shoes." She said, "I want to see them. Are they really pretty?" I stood in the back of the church with my left foot in the air while Mary Ann felt my shoe from toe to heel. She agreed with John that they were indeed beautiful.

One of our teachers, Bonnie Glassmire, had a yacht which she had had sent down from the States. In reality, it was her father's boat, but it was kept in Balboa. From time to time, we'd be invited to go on the boat and always enjoyed being at sea. We also had many boating adventures with the sea scouts, but those will be mentioned later.

The island of Taboga was a place I loved to visit. It lay just off Balboa and was reached by boat. Years ago, it had a hospital for patients with TB, as it was thought the salt air might cure them. When we were there, it was possible to stay in one of two hotels. However, we could go and come in one day; it wasn't necessary to spend the night. There was a beach with excellent bathing. One had to be careful not to be out there too long because Panama lies near the equator and one could get a terrible sunburn. A professor from Pennsylvania State University had to be hospitalized when she got blisters all over her legs.

Many of our friends went to our church. One of the oldest members of the congregation was Mr. Worsley. He was a ship's chandler. It was said he cooked a pot of beans on the weekend, which he ate all week. I don't know how true that was. He drove an old car that had rusted through on the bottom. He put boards down to keep his feet in the car. One day, a young man asked him why he didn't buy a new car since he knew Mr. Worsley was rich. Mr. Worsley replied, "Young man, I have the money I have today because I don't waste money."

A teacher in our school, Frances Graham, had a finca (farm) in the interior of Panama. Once a year, she'd invite us along with the members of the ROTC to a pig roast. A pit was dug in her yard the day before the party, and an entire pig (about 200 or more pounds) was put in the pit. I think banana leaves or some type of leaves were put under and over the pig, and a fire was started. The pig needed to cook for about a day. I was never there to see the preparation so I don't know how the pig was prepared. All I know is that the cooked meat was delicious.

The beach below her house had black sand from which a Japanese company later tried to extract iron, although I think the venture was unsuccessful.

There was a handyman on Frances's farm who had a woman and children living with him. Frances found out he was not married to the woman, and she put pressure on him to marry her. She offered him furniture and other items until he finally gave in and got married. At that point, all hell broke loose because he had other children by other women. Now he had chosen one woman above the others, and they, therefore, would have nothing to do with him. Sometimes, it is better to leave things as they are and not put one's own beliefs in play.

Friday nights in the fall, we went to football games. We had only two teams, Cristobal and Balboa. There was a great rivalry between the two. The games were sometimes played in Balboa and sometimes in Cristobal. When the games were in Cristobal, we took the Panama Railroad across the Isthmus. Whenever there was a large crowd going, old coaches with kerosene lamps were used. At such times, we felt as though we were living in the 1920s. There were lots of insects (sand flies) in Cristobal, and one needed to use insect repellent before getting off the train.

Friends who were closest to us throughout the years were the Murphys, the Paynes, the Bondurants, and the Bakers. Glen Murphy was dean of the college when Chuck was the deputy superintendent of schools. Katherine taught at the high school with me. Their children, Julie, Tom, and Jim, were around our Jim's age. Clarence Payne was our minister at the Balboa Union Church. He and Rosita, his wife, keep in touch with me to this day. Anita, their daughter, was in Jim and Lina's wedding. Tragically, their son David died a few years ago from cancer he acquired from solvents used to get grease off his body after he fell into the Panama Canal while canoeing.

Ken Lake was a psychology professor at the college. He and Chuck shared many interests and took trips together. Ken helped us put on psychology workshops, which Chuck and I attended. Edith, Ken's wife, was an artist who worked in ceramics. I have some of her pieces in my home. Their children were a bit younger, and I didn't know them as well.

Gene Bondurant worked at the high school with me, and his wife Jane was a counselor. Gene and his family came to Panama the same year we did. They live near us here in Greenville because this was Jane's hometown. I attend meetings of the National Association for Retired Federal Employees and see them there.

John Baker was the family court judge in the Canal Zone. He and his wife Jean lived down the hill from us in Ancon. Their two daughters were in school with Jim. After retirement, they moved to Maine where we visited them often.

Another interesting person we got to know through our church was Ambassador Wong. He was the ambassador to Panama from Taiwan. He had served with General Chiang Kai-shek and had saved his life. He invited the entire church to his home for a Chinese dinner, which we all enjoyed.

Buying Our Food

Much of our food arrived by ship from the United States. We could, nevertheless, buy fish locally as well as fruits and vegetables. The fishing fleet came into the wharfs. We would go there, pick out a corvina or red snapper, and the fishermen would clean it, filet it, or cut it into steaks. It would then be wrapped in newspaper to be carried home. Since we bought the entire fish, we got the head included. Elena, our Jamaican laundress, came on Saturdays. She liked to make fish soup. She would put the head in, and during the cooking process the eyes would float in the broth. Chuck made the mistake of saying he liked the soup. Finally, he told me to tell Elena he didn't want the head included because he didn't like eyes in his soup.

We got fruits and vegetables from the Chinese gardens. Certain Chinese families had been living in the Canal Zone for many years. They were allowed to stay and sell produce either produced by them or purchased. We could get watermelon, papayas, oranges, bananas, grapefruit, mangoes, and pineapple. Many types of vegetables were available including tomatoes, carrots, cabbage, yams, yucca, and plantains. The story is told that the Indians who raised the boguete oranges (large naval ones) would carry the oranges back home if they didn't get the price they thought they should get. The oranges were carried in large sacks on their backs. Mary always enjoyed going to the Chinese garden with me because she was always given a free banana.

Elena's Husband

Elena, our laundress, lived just outside the limits of the Canal Zone. Her daugher, husband, grandchildren, and a male friend lived with her. Elena's husband had worked for the U.S. government and got a pension. Apparently, she enjoyed his pension, as she always told me she wouldn't look for another man because she was married to Uncle Sam.

One afternoon, she came to the house and told us her husband Jim had been struck by a hit-and-run driver, and he was dead. She needed cotton and other supplies to prepare his body for burial. We were to take her and her family to the cemetery. The day of the funeral, we parked the car near the gravesite. Her minister was there. He began preaching in a hypnotic tone, at which point, Elena began swaying. She grabbed me, and for a minute, I feared I'd land on top of the coffin. She weighed over 200 pounds, and I was no match for her. Fortunately, Chuck grabbed me just in time, and both Elena and I stayed out of the grave.

Christmas On The Isthmus

Christmas was celebrated in a great way in the Canal Zone. The governor always held a tremendous party at his residence. One Christmas, my cousin Isabel came. She wanted to know how many formals and how much jewelry to bring. In those days, we really dressed up in long dresses with our best jewelry. I can't recall how many dresses Isabel brought, but I do know she had a splendid vacation with us.

Since many friends were alone in the zone, we made a point of inviting them for Christmas dinner. Sometimes, we had 50 people present; Emma, Tina, Elena, Carlos, and little Elena helped. Sometimes, people brought food, and sometimes we supplied it all. We had ham and turkey with all the trimmings. I made pecan, mince, and pumpkin pies. People usually came at noon and stayed until late afternoon.

Getting a Christmas tree was quite an ordeal. We were told what day the trees would arrive by ship. On the appointed day and time, the gates to the area holding the trees would swing open, and each person rushed in and grabbed a tree. We could peer over the fence and decide which one we wanted to buy. When two people chose the same tree, one had to back off and choose another. Not all the trees were perfect, but we were lucky to get one at all.

Christmas Eve was always celebrated with a service at church. At the end of the service, each person received a candle, which was then lit. We passed out of the church to the grassy hill surrounding it. There, we placed our candles until the hill was alight with burning candles. This was a tradition going back to World War II. Special permission had been given to break the blackout on Christmas Eve. Members of the church continued to do this year after year.

One Christmas, several of our guests got the flu. We had a house full of folks in bed. Fortunately, we knew Dr. Ramundo, and he was called upon for advice. Some had to wait a week before they could return home.

There was an elderly German man named Herr Mueller who taught at the college. On Sunday nights, he came to our house for supper. He called himself the "Tee Unkle." When Christmas came, I was often too busy to wrap presents. Herr Mueller would do it for me. One year, he gave me a plaque which read "Come in, sit down, relax, converse, our house doesn't always look like this. Sometimes it's even worse." Herr Mueller died in the Canal Zone and is buried there. In the end, he had thoughts that the Gestapo were out to get him. We often wondered what he did during the war. We understood he had married the daughter of the chief of police in Paris and had children throughout Europe. I understood that the children were contacted when he died, but they wanted nothing to do with him. Rumor had it that he had a Panamanian girlfriend.

Unopened Presents

One Christmas Eve, a huge fire broke out in the old section of Panama where there were many people crowded together in wooden tenements. Someone had lit a candle, which must have fallen over onto the floor during a power outage. The wood in the buildings is old and dry, and any flame causes it to burn. As the fire spread, people grabbed what little they had and rushed to safety in the Canal Zone. There was a large gas tank in the area, which people were afraid might explode. Chuck got a call in the late evening (probably 11 p.m.) from a man, asking him to open up the gymnasium to give the people a place to stay and to allow the Red Cross to set up a field station. Jim went with him to help.

The two were gone until three or four o'clock in the morning. They both were exhausted and fell into bed. They weren't ready to get up early in the morning to open gifts. In fact, I don't think they got up until nearly noon when our guests starting coming for dinner. We didn't want to open our gifts while our guests were there, and by evening, we were too tired. Our gifts were opened the next day when we celebrated a second Christmas.

If I remember correctly, the afternoon of the twenty-sixth, after opening the presents, Jim and Chuck helped the Air Force pack supplies to be sent to Guatemala because there had been a violent earthquake there. It was a Christmas that will never be forgotten.

Chuck and Alice flying from Panama to the States
for a vacation

Scouting On The Isthmus

Panama was the dropping off point for boats that would-be sailors found they no longer needed or wanted. Retirees who had never before sailed would get the notion they wanted to buy or build a boat and take to the ocean. This was how the Sea Scouts attained two of their boats, the Chief Aptakisik, a schooner, and the Mandala, a ketch.

One year, the scouts were given a 63-foot concrete schooner that had been built on one of the Great Lakes by a man and his son. They were not sailors, but they envisioned sailing around the world. In a storm in the Pacific, she lost her rudder and was adrift. Another ship came to her rescue and took her in tow. Their intent was to take her to Panama and claim her as a ransom for rescuing her. Somehow, she managed to get to the Canal Zone instead, and her skipper asked if there were Scouts who could use her. The matter was taken to court, but before the case was heard, Chuck asked to see where the ship had been when it was rescued. Since the rescue ship's compass was not working correctly, the reading placed the rescue on a mountain in Panama. The case was thrown out of court, and the Scouts got the ship. After we left the Zone in 1976, she sailed to New York to be in the tall ships parade, and a group of Scouts had a wonderful adventure. Chuck helped raise money for the trip.

Chuck became the leader of the Sea Scouts, which meant he spent most weekends either working on the boats or going on trips with the scouts. Sometimes, I felt like a ship's widow. The boys would go to Taboga Island or the Perlas Islands. Sometimes, Mary and I went along, and sometimes, we stayed at home. One afternoon, when Mary went but I didn't, she fell overboard. The waters were known to be infested with sharks. Chuck had instructed the boys in what to do in the event anyone fell overboard. When he heard the splash and Mary called, "Get me Daddy," he called for a drill, and the boys got Mary aboard within two minutes. I was just glad I didn't go that day.

Each year, in April, the Sea Scouts had a cayuco race. A cayuco is a Native American dugout canoe. The Indians cut down a tree and fashioned it into a long canoe. The Scouts would purchase one and adapt it to make it more competitive for a race through the Canal. The race took place over three days. The boys would leave from Atlantic side of the Canal to stay overnight near Gatun Locks. Then, they would continue to Gamboa the second day and the Pacific side the third day. The first cayuco to reach the Rodman Naval Station was the winner. The Scouts would work on their boats for months, trying to make them comfortable, using foam or whatever else they could find to pad them. Each group came up with some outlandish name for their boat. Jim's was called The Grapes of Wrath. One time, Jim made an important discovery. He found that if all the boys didn't row in unison, the boat would go around in circles. I find this is true many times when a group is trying to reach a goal!

One New Year's Eve, we decided we'd take a group of former Sea Scouts, Jim and his friends, to Flat Top, a small barren island near the mouth of the Panama Canal. The idea was to have a safe place to celebrate New Year's. The fellows helped the girls climb onto the island. I think Chuck, Mary, and I stayed on the boat. Everyone had a fine time, and we didn't come in until morning. That is one evening none of us will forget.

There was a time after Jim left for the university that made me wonder if I'd live to see him graduate. It was October, the time of "October Swells" in the Bay of Panama. This is a time when waves come from all directions, and they can be 20-30 feet high. When we started out, I don't think we expected any trouble. The trip began well; the seas were calm that afternoon and remained so overnight. Suddenly, the sea became very rough, and the waves increased in size. The boat would get in a trough, and we would see a gigantic wave with mountainous white caps coming our way. Chuck got so seasick, he just lay down and was unable to help command the ship. I put my arms around Mary and around the mast. If we had fallen, we probably would have gone overboard, and no one would have been able to rescue us. We could hear bells from either buoys or ships ringing in the distance. The storm kept up all day and all night. Fortunately, the boys were capable and managed to keep the ship afloat. Twenty-nine hours passed from the time we left the dock before we were able to return to the Zone. I thanked God we had made it safely home.

A European trip with friends and family

Memories Of Panama Trips

One of the first trips we took after we arrived in Panama was to Bocas del Toro, Almirante, David, and Boquete. We flew from Panama City to Bocas del Toro to see the fishing port. From there, we went to Almirante where we got on a small train to go through a large banana plantation. We saw how the bananas grew and how they were protected from insects by green plastic bags. While we were riding through the plantation, a young boy came aboard the train, hoping to sell a turtle. He held the turtle by a rope, which was tied around its leg. A man in our group who was a professor at the University of Panama bought the creature.

After leaving Almirante, we flew to David where we boarded a bus for Boquete. The professor put the turtle on a rack over his head and held the rope while the turtle sat with its legs hanging through the rack. Every once in a while, the professor would poke the animal in the stomach with his cane. We hadn't gone far when the man made us stop so he could order candy to take home. After that stop, we had to stop again so he could order a saddle for his horse. By this time, the entire busload of passengers was getting furious. We were hot and tired – and anxious to get to the hotel and take a shower. Once again, he made the bus stop so he could order strawberries. After this stop, he again poked the turtle. Apparently, the turtle had had enough poking because he urinated all over the professor, who had to go to the rear of the bus and change his clothes. Everyone on the bus clapped and cheered. We felt he had gotten his just reward.

Portobello

When we first got to Panama, the road to Portobello had yet to be built. Portobello is an ancient city on Panama's east coast. The Spaniards who plundered gold from the cities along the west coast of South America would bring the gold to the western side of Panama. Then, they would take it across the Las Cruces Trail by pack animal to Portobello where it was stored until the galleons could pick it up and transport it to Spain. English pirates plied the coast of Panama, hoping to capture the ships that were taking the gold to Spain.

One weekend, a party of Zonians decided to see if we could reach Portobello by fording the rivers that lay between Panama City and Portobello. The Lakes had an RV, which was large and high above the ground. We had a Volkswagon, which was supposed to float. We reached the first river, and Chuck drove the VW into the water. At first, the car floated, but gradually, it began to sink. Fortunately, we had rope with us. The men and boys waded into the water, tied the rope around the car's axle, and pulled it out. Ken and his crew did manage to ford the first river, and all 13 of us crowded into his RV to ford the next river. The second one proved too deep, and the entire trip was aborted. When we returned to the first river where we had left the car, it didn't start at first, but after being pulled behind the RV for part of a mile, the engine came back to life, and we were able to drive back home.

A trip to New Orleans for a counseling association meeting

First Trip On The
Inter-American Highway

In 1966, the Inter-American Highway, which was to link Panama with the U.S., was almost complete. The journey of 4500 miles led from the Canal Zone to the Texas border. Side trips to scenic vistas could add another 1000 miles. The highway was two-laned with three unpaved stretches: one of 60 miles in Panama; one of 150 miles in Costa Rica; and one of 25 miles in Nicaragua. At this time, the bridges had been put in, and it was no longer necessary to ford the rivers. The unpaved roads, however, resembled riverbeds with large and small boulders strewn on the road. One needed heavy-duty tires and springs on the car to travel those roads.

Teachers are known for carrying paper clips in their pockets, and Chuck was no exception. In Costa Rica, a paper clip came in handy when a cotter pin holding the rod that connects the shift lever to the transmission fell out, and we couldn't shift gears. Jim climbed under the car and discovered the problem. Chuck took a paper clip from his pocket, straightened it out, and replaced the cotter pin with it. It worked well and wasn't replaced until we got to Mexico.

After school was out, we put a trunk on top of our

station wagon and headed for Texas – and later, South Carolina. We followed a written plan that included information about where to find gasoline, restaurants, and hotels. It also listed points of interest along the way. In Nicaragua, for instance, we stopped to buy embroidered shirts for Chuck.

We had some adventures as we travelled. In Guatemala, we were suddenly surrounded by a group of men dressed in khaki who were carrying submachine guns. They demanded we take the trunk off the top of the car and open it. Chuck told them in Spanish that we were Americans and showed them our passports. He wouldn't take the trunk down. I was afraid we might be shot, but fortunately, after what seemed like an hour, they let us go. We never knew whether they were guerillas or Guatemalan soldiers at a checkpoint.

I also remember stopping in Chicastenango, Guatemala, to visit the cathedral. I saw Indian women in beautiful handwoven clothes entering the church. Once carried a live chicken. Apparently, chickens were not supposed to be in the church; she suddenly tucked the bird underneath her blouse. I wondered if it scratched her!

In Mexico, we were going up a hill and over some railroad tracks. As we were crossing the tracks, the car bottomed out, and the tires lost traction. Since we couldn't move the car, we had to find several men to lift it off the track.

We carried small packages of cereal in the back of the car, and they were visible from the back window. Near Oaxaca, Mexico, we encountered Indian women selling black pottery. One woman saw the cereal and wanted to trade some of her pottery for it. I still have a black angel I got from her in exchange for a box of Frosted Flakes.

During the summer of 1968, Chuck attended a workshop connected with the University of Pittsburgh. Part of the time was spent in Pittsburgh and part of the time in Guatemala. I was allowed to go with Chuck.

We had one interesting day that I remember. We were to visit a school in a village at the top of a mountain. We went to the bus station and got on the bus. The bus then went to a filling station to get gas. We took off. Apparently, the clutch didn't operate correctly, as we had a teenager beside the driver sitting on the floor, holding the clutch in place. We proceeded up the narrow road lined with crosses where unlucky drivers had gone off the edge of the road. The driver had a sign over his head that read: "With God's help, we'll make it." We hoped He was with us. We finally reached the village. The driver then said, "That was some road. This is the first time I've ever driven here."

We finally finished our visit, and the driver got us back down safely. I guess God was with us that day. Maybe He was there, because we had a nun in our group who delighted in wearing a red Guatemalan apron over her black habit.

Europe 1970

Our vacation in 1970 took us to Karlsruhe where we stayed in the apartment of a friend. From there, we went to Austria, France, Spain, Morocco, Gibraltar, and Andorra. We found we could live on five dollars a day per person. Going from Algeciras in Spain to Morocco by ship, we heard splashing and watched as packages wrapped in waterproof paper were thrown overboard. We then watched as small boats came from shore and collected them. Smugglers were at work. When we were ready to disembark, the women went into the restroom, tore the paper off bags of sugar and other commodities, and stuffed the individual items inside their large caftans. Evidently, they had pockets sewn inside. As we left the ship, everyone pushed and shoved like a bunch of chickens. I believe some never went through customs.

We returned to Karlsruhe and then headed to Scandinavia. We visited Finland, Norway, Sweden, and Denmark before returning to Germany. Jim was with us on this trip.

Finland was largely unpopulated, except for the cities. The train we were on travelled through the night. Since we were in the Land of the Midnight Sun, it was light all night. We had a compartment with three bunks. Jim was on the top one, I was in the middle, and Chuck was on the bottom. Chuck snored, and every once in a while, Jim would say: "Dad, roll over." Chuck would obey, and the snoring would stop for a while. This continued all night. Finally, when Jim repeated this again, Chuck replied: "You roll over. I'm tired."

When we reached the top of Finland near the Arctic Circle, we got off the train and had to walk over the border to Sweden to catch another train. We reached Narvik, Norway, late at night. We had no reservation at a hotel. A man from the train went with us around the town. Where there was a light, he called and asked if they had a room. We finally got one. Our beds were like large boxes with sides to keep out the cold. I felt as though I were in a coffin. We continued our trip through Norway, Sweden, and Denmark back to Karlsruhe.

In the summer of 1972, Jim went to Europe with the Rice Chamber Orchestra as a violinist. The group performed in Stade, Hamburg, Bremen, and Muenster. We flew over to hear the group play. One afternoon, Jim got locked in the bathroom of the farmhouse where he was staying. After some time, when he didn't appear for coffee, his host came to check on him. I'm not sure how he got out, but I remember his host told him the door hadn't been locked in years. After the concert tour, Jim went to work at Oak Ridge National Laboratories, and we flew back to the states with Icelandic Air.

We visited our Icelandic friends and persuaded their son to fly back with us. While with us, he enjoyed watching television and was most intrigued by the ads. He couldn't understand why we had commercials about toilet paper. We showed him New York at midnight. He couldn't understand why so many people were still up and about. After leaving New York, we took him to Pennsylvania where Chuck was to teach a course at the university. He stayed a few days and then went to California.

It was our custom, when we travelled extensively, to rent a car in France or Germany. The car was always new, we had the option to buy it if we wished. The year Jim was on tour, we rented a Simca. We had no intention of buying it. At this time, Rita and Atilla, whom we had sponsored, were living near Frankfurt. Atilla had an engineering job, and Rita was working for Rosenthal Fabrick. The company had a shop where one could purchase crystal seconds for a reasonable price. Rita mentioned this to me and suggested I go to see if I wanted to buy any bowls or glasses. She told me I could also get her discount.

I love beautiful glassware and decided I'd look to see what was on sale. I got carried away and bought enough objects to fill a huge carton. We put the carton in the car's trunk and left the plant. Sometime later, I began to question how we were going to ship our crystal to Panama. It would be very costly to have it correctly packed and shipped. When I asked Chuck for any suggestions he might have, he replied, "Well, we could purchase this car, put the crystal in the truck, and then lock the trunk." We did just that. We didn't give the shipping company the trunk key, and the trunk was never opened. All of our crystal reached Panama safely—with not one piece chipped or broken.

We used the car for several years, as it was small and

got excellent gas mileage. In the end, we sold the car for more than we paid for it. The next owner used it for many years and had no problem with it. We were pleased we had been able to purchase the car, because it became not only a means of transportation, but also a shipping container. How can one beat that?

Our Trip To Machu Picchu

The year after our adventure in Europe, when we purchased the Simca, we took a trip to South America. Our first stop was in Bolivia. The airport is on the Altiplano at 14,000 feet. We then went by bus down to La Paz, which lies in a sort of a bowl. It is at a much lower altitude. We hadn't been there long when Chuck got a terrible headache and began vomiting. We had been given coca tea to help us adjust to the change in altitude. It worked for me, although I had a dull headache for two days. It didn't work for Chuck. As he got sicker, I became frightened and went to the hotel reception desk. The clerk asked what the matter was. When I explained, he handed me a small cylinder of oxygen with a face mask. He told me to put it over Chuck's face and let him breathe the oxygen. Evidently, the altitude sickness happened frequently, and the hotel was prepared. After about an hour, Chuck began to respond. He used up the oxygen and was able to function well the rest of our trip. I learned Chuck did not do well at high altitudes, and we limited our future trips to places at lower altitudes.

After a couple of days in La Paz, we crossed Lake Titicaca by boat. We stopped at Copacabana, a pilgrim stop, and then went by car to Puno, Peru (formerly a silver mining town). We stayed in a small hotel in Puno where we could look down from our window to see the market. Puno looked like some Western town in the U.S., as it might have been in the early twenties. In the morning, we walked around the market. I remember seeing one man with a rooster tied to his leg. The rooster had the same expression on its face as the man; both looked as though they had had too much coca.

As we walked about, we saw a wagon covered with colorful handwoven scarves. I thought I would buy a couple. Chuck began pulling them off to see which ones we wanted to buy. As we got down to the sixth or seventh one, we found a baby sound asleep. The mother became very angry, as she thought we'd awaken her baby. We wondered why the baby didn't suffocate. At any rate, we chose two scarves from those on top of the baby and went on our way. Other lands and other customs!

From Puno, we took a train to Cuzco. It was extremely cold on the train, and we were glad we had warm clothing. Men came on the train selling woolen hats with ear flaps, along with blankets and food. We saw evidence of Inca trails as we proceeded to Cuzco. We took another train from Cuzco to Machu Picchu. Later, we discovered someone had gone through our suitcases, although they were locked, and I lost a manicure set and my travel clock. We reached Cuzco safely and took a bus to the hotel at Machu Picchu. The bus navigated fourteen hairpin turns before reaching the top. Lights went off in the hotel at 9 p.m. to save electricity.

In the morning, Chuck and a group of men decided to climb the mountain facing our hotel. There was a trail to the top. They hadn't quite reached the top when Chuck saw an Indian running toward them. The man didn't speak any English, but Chuck figured no one would run up the trail if there weren't an emergency. The man indicated they should descend. They went down and returned to the hotel. A landslide had caused a huge boulder to roll down the mountain and sever the railroad track, which we were supposed to travel on. A train took us to the break. We then got off that train with our suitcases and walked to another train, which took us to Lima and our flight home.

Alice Latimer, right, with daughter Mary, center, on a cruise
with her cousin, Edna Baldwin

Mother Latimer (Chuck's mother) with her grandchildren

Alice's sister-in-law, Betty, with husband Fred Dobey and daughter, Barbara

Alice and Chuck Latimer's niece, Candace, who accompanied them on some of their trips

Alice and Chuck Latimer's niece, Lauren, who accompanied them on some of their trips

Chuck's niece, Carol, mother of Lauren and Candace

Chuck Latimer with his aunt, Edith Eppes

Alice Latimer's English cousins, Gordon and Madeline
Perkins, with Virginia Emerson of Florida (center)

Alice, pictured with Ed and Dot, received the Verne Smith
Award for her work with the handicapped.

Alice Latimer with her first great grandchild, Sam, son of Ed
and Morgan Latimer

Costa Rica

One summer, we decided to spend a month in San Jose, Cost Rica, studying Spanish at the Instituto de la Lengua Española. Mary was with us. I went to classes in the morning while Chuck stayed with Mary, and I stayed with her in the afternoons while Chuck went to class. The school was really for missionaries who were going into Spanish speaking countries. We used the Spanish version of the *Good News Bible* as our textbook. The students were doctors or teachers. One man was very annoyed that we were using the *Good News Bible* because his church didn't believe that was the true word. I guess different people believe different things.

After our Costa Rican stay, we flew to the States and visited locations in Canada including Banff, Glacier National Park, and Lake Louise. The scenery was magnificent.

A Second Trip OnThe
Inter-American Highway

The year 1977 turned out to be a year with much travel. We left the East Coast after flying up from Panama and drove to Los Angeles. I assume we had purchased another car, but I have no recollection of the make. Jim joined us for a trip sponsored by Western Illinois University to Australia, New Zealand, and Tahiti.

We went on to Australia where we visited Katoomba and Canberra, and from there, we visited the north island of New Zealand. It was cold in Auckland. I remember the central heating in our hotel room was a small fan and a heater in one corner of the ceiling. We got hardly any heat at all from this system.

We visited the Mâoris and watched their colorful dances. We saw geysers and went into the Glowworm Caves. I was impressed with New Zealand and vowed to return to see the south island. On the way back, we were in Tahiti for Bastille Day, July 14. Nothing was said about any French activities that day. We decided to take a walk from our hotel to the center of town. When we got there, we found the governor and his new bride receiving gifts from different groups of Tahitians. Scantily dressed girls with flowering headpieces and coconuts or turtle shells for bras were dancing. Men carried stalks of bananas or a whole pig tied to a stick and presented them to the governor as bands played with fanfare. We returned to our group and told them they had missed a great show.

We returned stateside and began our trip back to Panama. Jim had gone back to school. We drove through Mexico, visiting parts we had not seen before. One interesting place we visited was Pancho Villa's home. The bullet-ridden car in which he was killed was still parked outside of the house in a glass enclosure. His widow, who was much younger than he was, still lived there, and we had a chance to talk to her.

While passing through Solola and Tecpan, we saw the results of the previous year's earthquake. We stopped at a local restaurant to eat lunch, and man approached our table and asked if he could join us. He was an American who had driven his tractor trailer down from New Orleans with his wife in order to help with the restoration of the cities. After several months, his wife returned to the States because she couldn't adjust. Apparently, he was very lonely, and he wanted to be with folks who spoke English. He asked if we would spend the night with him in his trailer and if I would cook a meal for him. At first, I wondered if we should do that, but we decided he was harmless and agreed to stay with him.

He had been invited to attend the opening of a small church he had helped build, and we accompanied him there. On the way, I sat with him in the cab, and Chuck sat on the trailer. We bounced over fields until we reached the church, which had wooden benches and was decorated with blue and pink balloons, a strange choice for a church. A small orchestra was at the front of the church. Chuck and I had been driving since very early in the day, and it was now about 8 p.m. He sat down and promptly fell asleep. I was suddenly aware that the pastor was telling the congregation that the gringo would now speak to them. I leaned over and punched Chuck. He opened his eyes, and I told him he had to speak. Fortunately, his Spanish was good enough that he was able to stand up and offer a well-received talk about friendship and love to the group.

We returned to the trailer, and our host had ham, potatoes, and apples there. Although it was after 9 p.m., I made us a meal that we enjoyed, as we were starved by that time. As I recall, Chuck didn't get much sleep that night because the man continued to talk. When we left the next morning, we felt we had given one lonely man some companionship.

When we reached Leon, Nicaragua, we got into a terrible sand storm. Chuck had gone to check on the hotel room. Suddenly, the sky turned yellow, and everyone seemed to be leaving the streets. I thought a volcano had erupted. Chuck returned to say a sand storm was beginning and we needed to get to the hotel quickly. We ran to the hotel and got in just in time. The proprietors had packed towels around all the windows to keep out the sand. The storm lasted most of the night.

We were glad to get back to Panama after our long journey and to be reunited with Mary, who had remained at home.

Turkey and Israel

In 1978, we decided we would join a teachers group from New York for a month's study at Tel Aviv University in Israel. From Panama, we flew to Rome, and from there, we flew to Istanbul on our way to visit Henny in Izmir. We went by bus from Istanbul visiting Gallipoli, Troy, Pergamum, and Ephesus along the way. The bus ride was interesting. There was a hostess on board who served us tea and cookies. We stopped at a clean, attractive restaurant for lunch. We spent one night in a motel near Pergamum. We had a long walk from where the bus let us off to the motel. The motel was primitive with no screens in the windows. We endured some mosquitoes. In the morning, a farmer passing by with a load of vegetables gave us a ride to the bus. At least we didn't have to walk.

While in Istanbul, we visited Suleiman's Mosque, The Topkapi Palace, the Folk Art Museum, and a military museum. Turkey is a land full of art treasures.

I had told Chuck, "I bet Henny doesn't drive in Turkey," and I was correct. When we reached Izmir, she met us with a taxi and took us to their apartment. We stayed several days until Zia drove us to Marmaris where we could catch a boat to Rhodes. The boat we took was a small sailboat with a Turkish captain. It was a beautiful sunny day with calm seas. There was a small car parked at the stern of the ship, belonging to a French couple. When we reached Rhodes, we found the boat had to back into the pier. As a result, we had to slide through the car in order to leave the boat. As we left, a man came up to us and said he had a small clean hotel and would like us to stay there. He showed us our room, which was clean and comfortable. We agreed to stay and were happy when he found us a good place to eat and a rental car. Both the restaurant and the car rental agency were owned by members of his family. We went to a light show on the Crusader's Castle and to a wine festival.

We finally reached Tel Aviv and found we shared a suite with Ruby and Jack Cohen. We got along so well that we have remained friends for many years. Ruby has since died of cancer, but Jack and I keep in touch.

Our classes took place Monday through Friday with tours on the weekends. We visited the Golan Heights, a tell, a kibbutz, and Masada. The visit to Masada took place at 8 a.m. when the temperature was already 112 degrees. I got to put my feet in the Dead Sea and had a church service with a British group by the garden tomb.

One weekend, Chuck and I decided to go to Haifa to see the Baha'i Temple. We left Tel Aviv on the last bus to go before the Sabbath. We enjoyed Haifa, especially the temple, which, as I recall, had a golden dome.

We returned to Tel Aviv on the first bus coming back after the Sabbath. The driver let us off at the bottom of the hill leading to our dorm. We walked back to our dorm carrying our suitcase. That night, we heard someone trying to get into our suite, but our door was difficult to open, and no one got in. Chuck thought someone might have been drunk and couldn't find his own room.

At breakfast the next morning, all of the group members were saying, "Wasn't it terrible? I was scared to death!" We asked what was so horrible and were told that Israeli soldiers, bare chested and wearing shorts, had broken into their rooms and stood over them with guns. The soldiers said they were looking for two Arabs who had been seen the previous afternoon walking up the hill with suitcases. We wondered whether we might be the reported Arabs. I'll never know.

When I think of Israel today, I think of the way the people have turned a desert into a land of beauty. When we arrived at the university, there were no trees, grass, or flowers. Several days later, large trucks appeared carrying palm trees, grass, and flowers. When we got back to the dorm in the afternoon, we hardly recognized the place. Grass and trees had been planted and flowers were blooming in profusion.

Sometimes, our professors didn't come to class. We would learn later that they had had to go on a military mission after a portion of Israel had been bombed. The people of Israel have been a brave lot to live under the constant tension of war. I too feel for the Palestinians and hope someday the two groups will come together in peace.

I Discover Art

No one in my family is an artist, and I never thought I could draw. When I was in grade school, I tried drawing an object and was laughed at. A few years before I left the Canal Zone, an art teacher at the college suggested I take her course. She said everyone could learn to draw. At first, I protested, but she persisted. I finally decided to take the class and to my surprise, I discovered I could draw. I now have many pictures to prove it.

Jim and Lina Marry Three Times

Jim met Lina through a mutual friend on a group date. He had his pilot's license and was a member of the Caltech Flying Club. Jim flew Lina and two other friends to the Red Baron Inn for dinner. Jim thought his friend was dating Lina, but he later found that this wasn't so, and the two of them began dating. Lina's visa was about to expire, and she needed to return to Indonesia. She asked if she could stop in Germany and visit her sister and brother-in-law on the way, and her request was granted.

At this time, Jim was working for Hughes Aircraft Company. Since he had attended a German gymnasium (school) for a year, he spoke German. Hughes was looking for an American engineer who spoke German to send to Ulm because Telefunken was having trouble meeting the specifications for the manufacture of satellite parts. Jim's name was mentioned as a possible candidate.

When Jim was asked, he accepted, and within a month, he was on his way. Once he reached Germany, he contacted Lina, and they were soon dating on weekends. Lina's sister and brother-in-law approved of Jim, and they told her parents that they did. Her mother soon flew to Germany and gave her approval for them to get married. They were first married in a civil ceremony in Germany on September

7, 1979, which happened to be the anniversary of my wedding to Chuck.

A Christmas Wedding

They made plans to have a wedding in Panama in the Balboa Union Church in late December. Lina needed an American passport, and arrangements were made for her to get one in California when she and Jim came back from Germany. When they reached California, her papers were nowhere to be found. Fortunately, the head of security at Hughes had once worked with the FBI, and he was able to cut through all of the red tape. A judge was called out of a Christmas party to swear in Lina as a citizen, and she was able to pick up her completed passport in Miami the morning of her flight to Panama.

Lina brought her dress from Germany, and Isabel and I made her veil. I can still recall sitting on the sofa with Isabel sewing the veil on the headpiece. Getting flowers in Panama in December is always a problem. In Panama, Mother's Day comes early in the month of December, and – other than chrysanthemums – most flowers are sold out. In 1979, the problem was compounded by riots in protest of the Shah of Iran. Lina wouldn't use chrysanthemums because they are used for funerals in Indonesia. I finally decided I'd get my friends to give me their red ginger, which was blooming in Panama at the time, and I'd use them to decorate the church. I gathered enough flowers to fill the trunk of our car and took them to a florist in Panama to make the bouquets. I found someone from whom I could buy orchids, and those were used for corsages and Lina's bouquet. Anthurium were used for the bridesmaid bouquets. Lina's attendants were Mary, Julie Murphy, and Anita Payne. Dale Prouty came down from California to be Jim's best man, and Brian Hoare and Bill Duffus were ushers. The daughter of one of Chuck's principals was the flower girl.

The Rev. Walter Reitz married the bride and groom. We had invited all of our friends, and that meant the church was packed. A large reception was held at the Quarry Heights Officers Club with about 200 people attending. We had an orchestra and a delicious buffet. I thought Jim and Lina would never leave for their hotel in Panama. I later learned that the custom in Indonesia is that the bride and groom leave last and parents visit them at the hotel.

The next day Jim, Lina, Dale, Louise, and Brian went to the San Blas Islands for a few days. They all reported they had had a wonderful time. While they were there, they observed a couple huddled together. Lina thought they might have been a professor and his student because of their obvious age difference. She asked the girl what they had been doing, and she said, "snorkeling." Lina thought she said *snuggling*, and she reported this to Jim. He laughed and said she hadn't understood correctly. She said – from what she had seen – snuggling made more sense.

An Indonesian Wedding

There aren't many couples who have had three weddings as Jim and Lina had. Their third one was in Jakarta. Lina's parents weren't able to attend the Panama wedding, and, therefore, wanted to host a ceremony in

179

Jim and Lina Latimer on their wedding day in Indonesia

Indonesia. Lina's stepfather is of Sundanese nobility and carries the title of "Raden," which is similar to the Indian title "Raja." Therefore, they decided on a Sundanese wedding reminiscent of the type the rajas had in the eighteenth and nineteenth centuries. It was held in the Ramayana Room of the Hotel Sheraton in Jakarta. Because this ceremony is not commonly performed today, a lady was hired to oversee the proceedings. She had been in charge of a similar event for an ambassador's daughter at the Indonesian Embassy in Washington.

We went to the hotel in the morning. We had a room with a balcony so that we could watch the preparations. Soon, men came with bamboo and orchids. While we watched, they made stands of the bamboo and intertwined the orchids at the top. Later, when it was nearly time for the wedding, I got into my sarong skirt, which was of rose pink and tan batik and my pink blouse. The blouse had been made after I sent a blouse from Panama to show the size. The shirt was made when I got there. I wore a black wig. A makeup team then came and put jasmine blossoms in my hair and put white makeup on me. Lina later asked why I had let them make me look so white. I thought they wanted me to look that way. Pictures from the wedding show me like a geisha girl.

A Sundanese wedding ceremony involves much symbolism. Since Indonesia has many Moslem people, it seemed to me that some of this was based on the Moslem religion. At first, the couple is greeted by the ceremony team, and the audience is asked to welcome them. Jasmine flowers are placed around their necks as a sign of welcome. The couple is then led to a place where the "sawer" ceremony will take place. Jim and Lina entered the room under a crimson silk umbrella, which was held by a young man. Lina's uncle greeted the crowd.

The ceremony starts with a song, which offers advice from the parents. A "harupat" (thin stick) is burned to symbolize avoiding strife and achieving a happy marriage.

Chuck and Alice Latimer at
Jim and Lina's wedding in Indonesia

A raw egg (no shell) in a plastic bag is placed on the floor; the groom is to step on it, and he must break the yolk. I was told a perfect man could break the yolk to make his wife happy.

Lina then had to wash Jim's foot with water from a Kendi (small jug). This shows she will serve her husband and control his steps, so he will follow the path God has shown him. After washing Jim's foot, Lina broke the Kendi to show that no handicaps would harm their marriage. Jim then had to knock on the door of an imaginary house to demonstrate that couples should show respect for one another. Lastly, Jim and Lina stepped over a barera (long stick) without touching it to indicate they would be alert about problems in marriage and avoid them.

The time came to seek Chuck's and my blessing; we held our hands in a praying position. Lina's mother and I threw coins and flower petals at the bride and groom. After this, we fed Jim sticky rice, and Lina's parents fed her. They then fed each other. This represented a break from their

Jim and Lina   Chuck and Alice Latimer at
                      Jim and Lina's wedding in Indonesia

parents and the start of a new life together. Cooked yellow rice, in a triangular form, represented a wedding cake. Jim was given an inscribed kujang (ceremonial curved sword) to guard his home. Unfortunately, it was later stolen from their California home.

During the ceremony, we sat on a dais in gold chairs with orchid stands behind us. Jim and Lina looked exotic in their surroundings. Jim had a jeweled turban on his head, and Lina had jasmine entwined in her hair. Their jackets and slippers were of crimson velvet embroidered in gold. The girls on the ceremony team were dressed in pastel chiffon dresses and reminded me of butterflies as they spread flower petals to show congratulations.

A reception followed for about 400 guests. A video taken at the reception shows Chuck and me bobbing up and down as we greeted each guest. As we thought about it, we realized the people were all shorter than we were, which meant we had to bow down to get closer to them.

The food served was plentiful and varied. We all ate until we were almost uncomfortable. The dishes ranged from Indonesian to European. The cake stood higher than Jim, who is six feet tall, and there was a fountain in the middle of it. We didn't realize a meal had been set aside for us in a separate room—which, in the end—none of us ate.

A room was set aside for all the floral tributes. As I recall, most of the flowers were orchids, which appeared to be like the colors of a rainbow. Many of the flowers had come from Singapore where orchids are cultivated. Sending flowers seemed to be more of a custom than gift giving.

After the wedding, most of the flowers went to the hospitals, and a few in baskets came back to Lina's family home.

Eddie, Lina's brother, rented a van, and Chuck and I, Jim and Lina, Eddie and his wife, and an Australian friend explored the islands of Java and Bali for two weeks. I was impressed by the tea plantations and Borobudur (a Buddhist shrine). The young women in Bali are slim and graceful as they walk carrying various articles on their heads. Indonesia is a tropical paradise, lush and colorful.

Good-bye To Panama

Our time in Panama was coming to an end. We were spending most of our time sorting through our effects, trying to pare them down to the 11,000 pounds the government would allow us to ship. In addition, we packed and mailed 7500 pounds of books, slides, and records.

There were luncheons, dinners, and other ceremonies to attend before we left – in July of 1981 – for the States. We hated to say "good-bye" to our loyal servants – Emma,

Both Chuck and Alice Latimer received gold medals
for community service from the governor
before leaving the Canal Zone.

Tina, and Elena – who had served us faithfully for 19 years. I was honored to have the annual Balboa High School Honors Assembly dedicated to me. Additionally, both Chuck and I received the Panama Canal Honorary Public Service Certificate and gold medal for our contributions to the community. We were especially honored to receive these; at the time, there were less than 24 recipients in existence.

Chuck, Mary, And Me: On Our Way Home

The three of us – along with 12 trunks – flew by military plane to Charleston, SC, where we left trunks with Chuck's parents and our friend Edna. After a night there, we flew to Denver where we picked up a new Dodge Omni. We attended a conference in Boulder. Then, we headed to California. We drove through Texas, New Mexico, and Arizona, visiting friends along the way. We spent four days in Azalea, Oregon, helping a friend pick and eat tomatoes, apples, pears, and blueberries. We also had an opportunity to visit Crater Lake where we saw snow.

We continued on to Portland where we spent a week. Our sightseeing included Mt. Hood and the restored fort where Lewis and Clark spent a winter. After Portland, we went to Seattle, and later, Port Angeles. From there, we sailed across the Juan de Fuca Strait to Victoria where we spent four days. One day, in Victoria, our car got towed when we got mixed up about a change in time.

From Victoria, we drove to Port Hardy where we took a British Columbia ferry to Prince Rupert. We spent four days there waiting for the Alaska ferry. We left our car and half our luggage at the Totem Motel before boarding the ferry. We enjoyed Prince Rupert with its fall foliage and snow-capped peaks. We had three sunny days in Ketchican, AK, which usually gets a lot of rain. We visited Juneau and had a short tour of Sitka en route.

We landed in Juneau around midnight. There were no taxis, and we had landed 12 miles from the center of town. Fortunately, a young priest from Los Angeles gave us a ride to the hotel. We spent five days there, seeing the Mildenhall Glacier and salmon spawning. Our ferry was out of service for repairs, but we caught a local one to Skagway. Since there were no staterooms, Mary and I slept on the lounge deck, and Chuck and the priest played cribbage all night.

Skagway was perhaps the highlight of the trip. The days were cold but clear, and there was a full moon at night. New snow glistened on the surrounding mountains both day and night. On Halloween night, light snow was falling on the boardwalk in front of the quaint 80-year-old Gold Rush hotel, "Golden North," which was filled with fascinating photographs and other mementos. We were the only guests – except for a female ghost on the third floor who was waiting for her lover to return from the Klondike. Townspeople came to the hotel for a costume party, and later, we walked to the nearby Red Onion Saloon (also a brothel in Gold Rush Days) to see girls mud wrestling in chocolate cake mix. We also broiled our own steaks at the Elk's Lodge and brought greetings from the southernmost lodge.

With the ferry still out of service, we left on the narrow-gauge "White Pass and Yukon Railroad." For $55 each, we were three of six passengers in the caboose behind a long train of ore cars, which had been emptied into a Japanese ship in Skagway. The train wasn't as fast as the one in Panama. It took seven hours to make the 110-mile trip to Whitehorse. However, the views were spectacular as we twisted upward 7000 feet to reach the mid-point of Lake Bennett where we, along with the train's crew, were fed Irish stew and apple pie. After a cold night in Whitehorse and a glimpse of Sam McGee's cabin, we boarded a Greyhound bus and travelled down the Alaska Highway through the snow to Prince George for another night of rest.

Our trip southward along the wild Fraser River down to Vancouver was characterized by good weather and beautiful scenery. After a pleasant weekend in Vancouver (where, in the maritime museum, we saw the "Saint Roch" that had made two trips through the Northwest Passage), we drove through Surrey to see Sue Emerick and her children before returning to Seattle in the rain.

We visited Chuck's cousin in Seattle for a day. Then, we proceeded to Long Beach where we spent Thanksgiving. After the holiday, Chuck flew east to help his parents get ready to move to Greenville – where they would be closer to us. He returned to Long Beach in time for us to celebrate Christmas with Lina and Jim and their friends.

In the middle of January, we began our trip east, visiting friends in Nevada, Arizona, Texas, Florida, and Alabama. We spent a month in Houston with Chuck's cousin Frances. Her husband had died after a long illness, and we were able to help her.

We arrived in Greenville in the middle of March in

1982 and soon were in our home, which we began renovating. I helped Chuck install an overhead garage door by stacking up books to raise it to the proper height. Fortunately, we had a lot of large books.

Starting Over In South Carolina;
Greenville – Our First Five Years

We made arrangements for Mary to attend a workshop offered at the Piedmont Skills Center. She looked forward to riding on the van each morning and to seeing her friends. The YMCA offered a swimming program for the handicapped, and Mary enjoyed it as well. Both Chuck and I volunteered and got to know many of the clients.

In order to make new friends, I joined an art group, which met weekly at a local bank. Most of the women were very friendly, and some were quite talented. Chuck and I helped each other. Both of us began to go to Mensa meetings, along with educational activities, military group meetings, and church functions. We joined St. Giles Presbyterian Church, which Mary had chosen when she saw the members having a picnic. Soon, we were as busy as we had been in Panama, and we felt at home. We enjoyed going to the many plays and concerts Greenville has to offer.

In July we became grandparents for the first time with the arrival of Edward. I went to be with Lina, as she had a C-section and couldn't do much for about a week. Ed weighed eight pounds, three ounces, and Lina is a small person. I was delighted to hold that beautiful child who had dark hair and eyes to match. At Christmas time, he was baptized at Lickville Presbyterian Church in lower Greenville County where some of his ancestors and Chuck are buried.

After we arrived in Greenville, we heard of a camp in North Carolina that Mary could enjoy while we travelled. Camp Sky Ranch is near Boone, NC, and Mary was happy there. In 1983, we made an eight-week, 15,000-mile auto trip from Newfoundland to California. We crossed 27 states and six Canadian provinces.

When I first returned to the States, I took an exam to become a registered dietician and passed it. Many were astonished that I could pass it after having been out of school for so long. I did, however, use a study guide to prepare for the test. In September of 1984, I started work at Greenville Memorial Hospital as a clinical dietician. I worked in the medical center clinic with patients sent to me by residents and staff members. I got to know many of the patients over a period of five years when I worked there. That was such a satisfying period of my life.

Chuck and I had planned to open a counseling practice in South Carolina, but we never managed to get one started. Sometime in 1984, Chuck was asked to got to Polk County, NC, to be their school psychologist. They wanted him full time, but he didn't want that because he wanted to be able to travel. In the end, he worked almost full-time, but his time off was extremely flexible. He often said the nine years he spent with the schools there were among the happiest of his life. The staff trusted him and followed his teachings. Under his watch, the schools in that area did away with the practice of paddling students.

One of the things we – especially Chuck – noted when we came here was that we were the ones who had to find a way to do whatever was needed when we volunteered for an organization. In Panama, Chuck's staff could always be called upon to help. I, of course, missed the help of our maids and our laundress. To this day, I tend to put off ironing.

We spent time each week volunteering with the handicapped. We went with a group of Mary's friends to the YMCA for swimming. Because we got to know these folks, we became guardians for two of them, Otis and Ann. For many years, both of them came to our home for the holidays and celebrated with our family. They have both passed away, and I really miss them. Otis died of cancer and Ann of a heart condition. In both cases, after their deaths, we became aware of family members they had who could have had contact with them.

In early January of 1985, we flew to Panama and stayed with friends for a couple of weeks. It was nice to return and to see how things were changing.

After we got home, the son of German friends came to visit, hoping to improve his English. He volunteered at the hospital and went with me to work. He wanted to drive each day, but that made me nervous. Chuck later said that when Ed and Richard wanted to learn, he'd do the teaching. He thought he would be better at it than I would.

That summer, we decided to fly Space A to New Zealand. A friend's daughter and her husband (a naval officer) were stationed in Christ Church and had invited us to visit them. We had been there about two weeks when they mentioned there was a flight going to American Samoa; they thought we might like to fly there. Of course, we did!

We arrived safely, explored American Samoa and Western Samoa where Robert Louis Stevenson had lived – and decided to fly back to New Zealand. There was only one plane a week flying in those days. We checked in and found we could get on board that flight. However, at boarding time, we were told there was a delay due to a storm. A naval officer who lived in Samoa invited us to his house for a sandwich while we waited for the storm to pass. We were eating lunch when we heard the roar of a plane's engine. Chuck said, "There goes our plane. I knew we shouldn't have left the airport." When we returned to the airfield, the plane had left, and our baggage was sitting where the crew had put it. The storm had passed quickly, and the crew had orders to fly.

What were we going to do now? We had a week to kill before we could get out. Chuck looked around and found there was an Air Manua plane that flew to and from one of the Manua Islands. Margaret Meade had conducted much of her research in this area. Chuck inquired whether there was any place to stay there and discovered there was a small hotel.

We flew out in a small plane, which skimmed over the water. I sat in the co-pilot seat. It was a beautiful day, and as I looked down, the water looked as though it were covered in diamonds. We arrived on the island and found a straw hut with a sign that said *Officini John*. John was there with his truck. He had only one hand. The right one appeared to have been cut off at the wrist. When no one from the hotel came to meet us, he volunteered to take us in his truck. It was amazing to see him shift gears with his stump of a right hand.

We arrived at the small hotel and found no one there. John had left us. We explored the hotel and found rooms with cots that were not made up, a bath, and a kitchen with a few food products. I saw rice and a rice cooker. Fortunately, with an Asian daughter-in-law, I knew how to use the cooker. In a short while, a tall young man appeared wrapped in a sarong type skirt. He pointed to the bedroom and said, "Sleep here." I asked where the sheets were, and he pointed to a closet. Chuck asked when we were to eat, and he replied, "No food." We said we understood we were to be fed, but he again replied, "No food," and left us. We had a peanut butter sandwich with us, so we knew we wouldn't starve that night.

Several hours later, a young couple arrived. They were from Australia and were on their honeymoon. They hadn't been fed either, but they had learned how to get food. They told us they were leaving the next morning, but they would help us get food.

When morning came, we were awakened by shouting and talking. We looked outside and saw a woman dressed like a nurse standing by a truck. There were men putting bedding in the back of the truck. A large woman was carried out and placed on the bedding. Chuck got dressed and went outside to find out what was happening. Another truck appeared with a dark-skinned man behind the wheel. The report Chuck brought back to me was that the chief's wife was having complications with her pregnancy, and she was to be air lifted to a hospital in Pango Pango. The dark-skinned man had come to take the Australian couple to the airport where they would fly to American Samoa to catch a plane home.

The driver agreed to come back to the hotel and take us to a store so we could pick up some basic supplies. He kept his word and drove us to a small store where we could buy cereal, milk, butter, and other items. We learned that the storekeeper was also the baker and the schoolmaster. He had been in the Marines and was one of the chiefs of the island. When he heard Chuck was a naval officer, he invited us to a feast at his home.

We learned that, on Ofu, all fresh food items were exchanged by barter. If I gave a person a fish, I expected to get bananas or some other food in return. We, of course, had nothing to exchange. Fortunately, we were given a parrot fish and some bananas. Later, when the owner of the hotel cooked food in a pit, we were given some of that. I learned to prepare bananas many ways: baked, boiled, fried, etc. We didn't starve while we were there. A doctor from Seattle stayed at the hotel for several days and joined us at mealtimes.

The chief, with his wife and another couple (the husband was also a chief), hosted a banquet for us. We had more food than we could ever eat. I could see why the people on the island were as large as they were. We were told the average woman weighed 250 pounds. I think the men must have topped 300. One of them told me he wouldn't want me for a wife because I was too small.

An interesting custom there was that generally, women did all the work. If a family had no daughter, a son was designated to take the place of a daughter, and he dressed as a woman. Whether that was true or these people were cross dressers, I don't know. I did, however, see at least two men dressed as women.

We enjoyed our week there. We spent a part of each day sitting on the lava in the ocean. The water came up over our waists. A myriad of tiny colored fish swam over our legs and all around us. We sat still, and they treated us as part of their natural environment. Living out in the middle of the Pacific Ocean was like a quiet sanctuary, but at the end of the week, I was glad to get back to American Samoa and from there, New Zealand.

After returning to Christ Church, I leaned over to get something from my suitcase and injured my back. My hostess took me to her doctor and later to a physical therapist who used heat and massage to get my back in condition to travel again. She did a good job, and we were able to explore the South Island. We saw sheep ranches, lakes, and forests filled with ferns. We visited Mt. Cook and the Franz Josef Glacier. Our trip came to an end, and we used a military flight to go back to the States.

Lina Latimer graduated from California State
University, Long Beach.

1986

On October 1, we moved into the house next to my in-laws. They were getting older and needed our help. Mother could also keep Mary in the mornings and afternoons when she wasn't in the workshop.

In June, Lina graduated from California State University at Long Beach with a bachelors degree in accounting. I was so proud of her. She had come to the States just eight years before – not speaking much English. She had gotten a degree from a college in Indonesia, but her studies were not in English. I can't imagine going to another country where I didn't speak the language and earning a degree. We celebrated her graduation in California.

Shortly after our return, Mary went to camp, and we took a military flight to Germany. We rented a car and went to Aachen and stayed with Renata and her family. Henny came from Turkey, and the four of us went to Ghent and Bruges in Belgium. We stayed at the Rembrandt-Rubens Hotel, which was 500 years old. We enjoyed watching the women make lace. We visited Karlsruhe and the Black Forest. We drove through France and Switzerland to Italy. We were surprised that a superhighway with tunnels had been built in Switzerland. This enabled us to cross

Switzerland in three hours with a $30 dollar toll. Thirty years before, it had taken two days to make the same trip.

We spent one week in Bergamo, Italy, which is a sister city to Greenville. We had met a couple from Bergamo when they were in Greenville, and they had invited us to visit. They lived in a beautiful apartment in the lower part of Bergamo. While we were there, we went to Pellegrino where the springs yield the water sold there, as well as in Greenville. We visited a monastery where our hosts' daughter, an artist, was helping to restore paintings. One night, we had a delicious dinner in the ruins of an old abbey. There were candles about six feet high giving light to our table.

When we left Italy, we continued on to Yugoslavia, as it was called then. We visited Split, Dubrovnik, Sarajevo, and Belgrade. We were happy we got to see these cities before war brought so much destruction. As we were leaving Yugoslavia, we had some money left. We stopped in a store and bought some brown and white blankets, which I think Jim and Lina still use. We returned to Germany through Hungary and Austria. We had covered 5000 miles.

The Second Five Years In Greenville: 1987-1991

Mary had lived at home for 33 years, but as Dad's health failed, Mother found it difficult to help with both Dad and Mary, so we had to find a home for Mary. I, of course, was working at the hospital. In November of 1987, I received a call; there was a place for Mary in one of the group homes. Mary adjusted well. The staff was wonderful, and we were joyful.

Since Mary was settled, we took the opportunity that summer to fly Space A from Seymour Johnson Air Base to Zaragoza, Spain. From there, we flew to Mildenhall, England. In addition to visiting my cousins near Bath, we visited friends. We covered a great deal of England including Ely, Huntingdon, St. Ives, Chester, Haworth, and the Isle of Wight.

1988

Dad's health continued to decline. His birthday was April 29. Chuck predicted he would make his birthday, but probably would not live long beyond that. He was correct. We had a huge birthday party with all his children and grandchildren present. Dad was bedridden and really wasn't able to comprehend all that was going on, but each person did get to say, "Good-bye and I love you." Dad died May 6 in the Veterans Hospital near Asheville, NC. He wanted to go there where his brother-in-law had once been the hospital administrator. After working in the depths of Navy ships as an electrician, he had gotten lung cancer from the asbestos found on the ships.

That summer, we took a trip to Canada, visiting Ottawa, Montreal, Quebec, and the area beside the St. Lawrence Waterway, as well as the Gaspe Peninsula. We stayed at B and B's along the way. When we returned home, we built a garage and added a bathhouse by the large pool that Mary and her friend enjoyed.

1989-90

We had planned to spend several weeks during the early summer months in China and Tibet. Because of the Beijing Massacre, we changed our plans and went to Hawaii, Australia, and New Zealand. One night in Australia, we had a space heater and heavy draperies over the windows in the room. Despite both of these, we were freezing and wrapped ourselves up in blankets. When we were leaving in the morning, I noticed the window behind the drapes was wide open. It had never occurred to me that it might not be closed.

In July, we flew to Germany, rented a car, and drove through East Germany, Southern Poland, Austria, Czechoslovakia, and Ljubljana in Yugoslavia. We stopped to visit Auschwitz on the way. We arrived in Ljubljana during a storm with hail the size of golf balls. The following morning, some of the balls were still on the ground.

In the spring of 1990, we visited the Canary Islands and spent a week on each one. While there, we received a call from Los Angeles that Richard, our second grandson, had been born. We were delighted. Richard was as beautiful a baby as his brother had been.

Each year, folks who have lived in the Canal Zone gather in Florida for a reunion. This usually takes place in early July, and there may be 2000 people present to recall old times. We went on a five-day cruise with some of them and attended the reunion.

In the summer, the International School Psychologists Colloquium was held in New Hampshire. Friends came from Port Elizabeth, South Africa, to attend and stayed a few days with us before going on to New Hampshire with Chuck. Shortly after they left, our friends from Bergamo, Italy, arrived, as there was a sister city convention in New Mexico. When Chuck returned from New England, all of us flew to New Mexico and rented a car. After the meeting there, we visited the Petrified Forest, the Painted Desert, the Grand Canyon, and Los Angeles. After leaving L.A., we drove to Phoenix, Albuquerque, and New Orleans where we left our friends and flew home. We had had a very busy summer.

1991

This was another year of travel. At Easter-time, we flew to Bermuda and spent a week there. We almost got killed. Good Friday in Bermuda is Kite Day. Someone had been flying a kite, which apparently had fallen, and the nylon string was stretched across the road. We were on a moped when Chuck suddenly put on brakes, and both of us slid off the vehicle. If he had not seen the string, he would have been decapitated, as it was at the level of his throat.

Before the residences for the handicapped came under state control, and when there was more money available, clients got to take group vacations, and parents could go along. In May, I went with Mary and her friends on a Carnival cruise. The group enjoyed swimming, and they loved the food.

Jean and John, friends from the Canal Zone, had a home in Castine, Maine. John had graduated from West Point and had been influential in getting a group of his classmates together each year in Maine. Chuck became an honorary member of his class, and we joined them for corn roasts and boat rides along the coast of Maine – a good way to avoid the South Carolina heat.

September found us in Puerto Rico for a week. When we returned, we found Mother ill. She had found a lump in her abdomen, but she had never told us. When she was seen by a surgeon, he said she needed an operation. Fortunately, she had a cyst – not cancer. I was supposed to clean the wound each day and redress it. The doctor scolded me for not rubbing harder, but I just couldn't bear hurting her. Mother had her ninetieth birthday in November. We invited all the family and told them to take all the furniture in the house back with them. Each one took what she had given Mother, and they divided the rest among them. Everyone was happy about the division.

When it was time for Mother to enter a residence, we chose Southern Oaks, a fairly new one. Edith and Alice, Mother's sisters, helped Mother make the transition. Mother understood I couldn't take care of her, but she didn't want to move. At the time she was to enter the residence, Chuck was away. Mother told me I wasn't her daughter, and I couldn't tell her what to do. I was glad Chuck returned and backed me up. Mother later apologized to me and said she was sorry she had spoken to me like that.

1992

I was kept busy this year as I served on both the South Carolina Dietetic Board and the Greenville County Disabilities Board.

During Spring Break, we flew to Ecuador and spent three days in Quito with a visit to Otovalo. The markets were colorful, and the people were friendly. From there, we flew to Guayaquil where we boarded a 95-passenger boat bound for the Galapagos Islands. We visited most of the 12 islands. We were there during mating season for birds and were able to walk within three feet of them as the male frigate birds stretched their red necks like balloons to attract the females. We saw sea lions, iguanas, penguins, boobies, and finches. We didn't, however, get to see the giant tortoises, as the keepers were on strike.

We went snorkeling on one of the islands. As I was swimming around with the fish, a pelican flew down right beside my head to scoop one up. It was on this trip that we met our close friends from England (now in Australia), Tom and Connie Parker.

When summer arrived, we again went to Europe to attend the International School Psychology Colloquium, which was held in Istanbul, Turkey. We invited my college friend Louise to accompany us, along with our grandson

Ed. We flew to Paris and picked up the Renault we had ordered. Then, we headed to Aachen to visit our friends. All of the roads around the airport were blocked with trailer trucks, and it took hours to get to Germany because of a French truckers' strike. We finally arrived around 2 a.m.

We didn't realize we were not supposed to drive in the Communist Block countries, as our insurance didn't cover us there. Fortunately, we did not have an accident. We left Aachen and headed east. We visited Giessen, Jena, Wittenberg, and Berlin. We then went into Poland and visited the Stansliks, whom we had met through correspondence, in Piła. We stayed at a little inn near their apartment.

At this time, the husband, who was an orthopedic surgeon, and his wife lived in a one-bedroom apartment. They had a new baby who got ill while we were there. They would have had to travel to the hospital by bus if Chuck had not been there to drive them. The doctor had to stay at the hospital when he was on call, as they had neither a car nor a telephone. The wife was a German teacher. When asked what we could bring them, he replied he wanted an anatomical atlas, and she requested a German-Polish dictionary.

We stayed several days there and got to visit Gdansk, Warsaw, Krakow, and Torun, the city where Copernicus was born. There was a dance festival in Krakow with dancers from all over the eastern countries wearing colorful costumes. Gas was scarce, and we had to wait in line over two hours to fill the tank of our car.

After leaving Poland, we drove through Hungary,

Romania, and Bulgaria before reaching Turkey. We spent one night in the mountains of Romania and met Scottish nurses who had come to care for Romanian orphans. An observation I made in Romania was that there was hardly any traffic except in the cities. Geese were waddling in the middle of the road. This was the time of the Yugoslavian war, and the truckers were taking the same route we were taking in order to avoid the war zone. They too were heading for Turkey and the near east. We had no trouble with the border crossings until we got to Bulgaria. At the Romanian border, the guard saw our American passports and said, "Americans, no problem." At the Bulgarian crossing, however, trucks were lined up for miles. We waited patiently for nine hours before we could cross. It was particularly bad because there were five or six gypsy children who had decided to make money. They threw dirty water on our windshield and then wiped it off with a dirty rag. One of them would then come to the driver's window, hand outstretched for money. This was repeated over and over. No one attempted to stop them.

After the long wait, we finally got across and drove until we came to Russe on the Danube. We had no hotel reservations, and all the signs were in Cyrillic. Fortunately, Chuck had studied Greek at the College of Charleston. He was able to read the word *Centrum*. We saw a police car parked by the road. Chuck got out and went to the car with his passport. He said, "Americans, hotel." The police indicated we were to follow them. They led us to a large beautiful hotel on the edge of the Danube. No one on the desk spoke any language we spoke, but gestures got us a room, and we slept well. In the morning, we ate our breakfast in the dining room and were surprised to find the entire ceiling of the room had been pulled back and we could see the sky. A huge bowl of apples was in the middle of the tables, and the waitress later presented them to me in a bag for our journey. Chuck tried to tell the girl on the desk that we appreciated the help of the police and would she thank them. The girl looked dumbfounded that we had been helped.

We had a problem in the last Bulgarian town, Hosnovo, before crossing into Turkey. We couldn't open the trunk. We knew the Turks would want it open and would think we were hiding something if it didn't open. Neither Chuck nor I was aware one could get into the trunk through the backseat.

Ed, however, in a period of boredom, had read the car manual. He took the seat out and climbed into the trunk. A carton of orange juice had gotten wedged under the trunk lock; once it was removed, the trunk opened. I can't recall what reward we gave Ed, but I'm sure he received one.

We spent about an hour walking around Hosnovo, which looked like one of our cities 100 years ago. The department store had glass display counters, but there were few items for sale. One counter had men's clothing. I saw only five or six shirts, a few ties, and some underwear. The grocery store had sacks of flour and sugar piled up with a cat asleep on several. I wondered where the rats were or if the cats had caught them.

After reaching Turkey, we drove up to Çeşme where

Zia and Henny have a summer home. We took dips in the hot springs near their home and enjoyed the small watermelons, which were brought daily to the house. We marveled at a hotel nearby which had been a Caravancerai and was hundreds of years old. It dated from the time when men traveled by camel, and these accommodations were placed 40 miles apart (as far as a camel could travel in one day). Our conference there was meaningful. We stayed at a small family-run hotel, The Vardar Palace. The manager liked Ed and paid him to help at the desk. At the end of our stay, he called California and told Jim and Lina that they had a wonderful son.

We left Turkey and took a ferry to the Greek island of Chios where we visited a monastery and watched grapes being pressed for wine. We visited Piraeus, Athens, Corinth, and Olympia (where the Olympics were first held). Another ferry took us to Brindisi and we began our trip through Italy. We stopped in Assisi to see a friend and visit the cathedral. Assisi is on a hill, and all around the bottom are parking lots. We parked the car and walked up to the top. It was 100 degrees that day. When it came time to leave, Ed said he'd go ahead to the car, and we could follow. Unfortunately, we got lost. Chuck said he'd walk around the base of the hill to find our car. After an hour, he returned about to collapse. Louise and I had stayed in one spot waiting. We finally found a policewoman who got us a cab, and we drove around looking for the car. At the last parking place we found it with Ed inside crying. Ed's remark was, "My mother told me to stay with you so I wouldn't get lost, but you stupid people were the ones who did." We had been gone well over an hour, and I guess he thought he'd never see us again. The parking attendant had tried to help him, but Ed couldn't understand Italian. Ed did get a big ice cream cone to make him feel better. We stopped at Bergamo and Dijon, visited friends, and then, flew home. While in Bergamo, we visited a chapel where old paintings were being restored. We all agreed we had seen things we couldn't have believed we'd see. I even saw a gypsy wagon with a bear standing on the back. I suppose the gypsies would put on performances with the bear.

1993

During Spring Break, we flew to Taipei to visit the island of Taiwan. My friend Ethel had tutored a young woman while her husband was a student at Bob Jones University. Ethel had put me in touch with her, and she and her family agreed to host us while we were there. We stayed, at first, at a small hotel near their apartment. We were comfortable there, but I was concerned because there was no top sheet on the bed, and I don't like to use bedding others have used without something clean between the blanket and me. After a couple of days, we were invited to stay with the family.

One of the first days we were there, we were invited to go to a Chinese grave sweeping. The family members go to the cemetery with food, firecrackers, brooms, and paper money. Food (later taken home) is placed on the grave, and the area around the grave is swept and cleaned. Everyone present is given a hard boiled egg to eat. After peeling the egg, the shell is crushed and spread on the grave. Paper money ($1000.00 worth of fake paper bills) was placed all over the grave. Lastly, firecrackers were set off. We could hear the noise from all over the cemetery. A small building was on each grave. After a certain number of years, the remains are taken from the grave, placed in a jar, and stored in the small house. After taking part in the grave sweeping, we went to a relative's home for a meal. A large pot with food boiling in water was on a table. We sat around it, using our chopsticks to take out food. We all shared the same pot of food.

We visited the National Palace Museum in Taipei and saw jade in a rainbow of colors carved into many different sculptures. Chinese handicrafts are intricate and exquisitely crafted. General Chiang Kai-shek is buried in Taipei, as is his son. We visited both sites. We also visited the beautiful Haroko Gorge.

George's brother was a physician at the hospital of the National Taiwan University. At the time we were there, his brother had recently been diagnosed with cancer. I found out he had gotten this disease as a result of a former Chinese custom. Mothers would chew food to make it

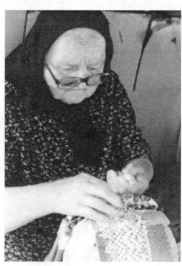

Lace making in Slovakia

soft and then spit it out and feed it to their infants. If a mother had hepatitis (which George's mother must have had), she passed it on to her child. This disease eventually turned into cancer. George himself was later to get cancer.

During our stay, we toured much of the island and got to visit temples, acrobatic shows, and native markets. In a fish market, I saw an eviscerated fish with the heart attached and still beating to show the fish was fresh.

The International School Psychologists meeting in the summer was held in Banska Bystrica, Slovakia. Along with Ed and our niece, Candace, we flew to London and got a Renault for our transportation. We drove to Dover and took the ferry to Calais. We stayed on French farms in Normandy and took Candace and Ed to see Omaha Beach (where the World War II landings took place), the Bayeux tapestry, which was made after the Battle of Hastings in 1066 A.D., and Mont Saint Michel. We visited friends in Belgium, Germany, and Poland before driving through Hungary to Banska Bystrica, Slovakia where our conference was to take place.

We spent a week at Matej Bel University. Students from the university helped with the conference. One student, Michel, became Ed's friend and took him home with him to meet his family. Michel was a help to us when we needed anything. One day, Chuck wanted a haircut. He asked Michel where the barbershop was. It became obvious Michel had never been to one, as he had to ask where it was. Chuck went there, and a woman cut his hair. When she finished, she charged him a small amount, maybe 75 cents, and then asked how much he would have paid at home. He didn't want to tell her the exact amount, so he said, "I guess I pay about three dollars." At which point, she said, "If I got that amount, I'd only have to cut a few heads a week."

Ice cream, expensive in most parts of Europe, was cheap here. There was an ice cream stand on the town square. The vendors sold a cone for three cents and a scoop of ice cream for four cents. Chuck told the two youngsters they could have as many scoops as they wanted. I envisioned them buying a skyscraper of a cone, but two or three scoops sufficed.

There were some good restaurants there. We took Michel's family to one as a treat. I don't think they went out to eat often. One Chinese restaurant where we ate had the ceilings done in red satin, so it looked posh, and the food was good.

After our conference, we drove to Bratislava and continued along the Danube to Melk and then to Lake Constance (Bodensee) to see the falls at Schaffhausen. We spent a night near Freiburg where we had spent our first weekend in 1957. We visited the Gazaignes and stopped to see the railway car where the armistice was signed at the end of World War I. We crossed the English Channel by ferry and stopped in Dover, where we visited a museum (no longer in existence) that recreated the bombing of London, complete with loud booms and shaking of the building. I'm glad I wasn't in the real bombings.

We visited Canterbury and saw a recreation of Chaucer's "Canterbury Tales." Ed remarked that if the story were told in high school as it really was, the students would pay more attention. We spent our last night in England in a Sussex farmhouse built from timbers salvaged from the Spanish Armada, sunk in 1588.

We had a fall trip to New England and Canada with Jim, Lina, Ed, and Richard, as well as a late fall trip to Hawaii where we visited Oahu, Hawaii, Molokai, and Maui.

1994

This was the year we visited South America rather than Europe. The International School Psychology group was meeting at the University of Las Campinas near Sao Paolo, Brazil. We left Los Angeles with Ed on July 11 and flew to Sao Paolo. From there we flew to Manaus where we spent two nights. Our next stop was Brasilia, where we spent another two nights. During this part of our trip, Ed had his birthday. We celebrated by hiring a boat and a pilot to cruise the Amazon. The pilot brought along fishing gear and some meat. He stopped where he knew there were piranha, and he caught several. We took them to a native hut where he cooked them for us to eat. There was a Brazil nut tree in the yard, which a native climbed to get us some nuts to accompany our fish. I learned later there are over 30 varieties of piranha, not all of which are flesh-eating.

We joined the ISPA members in Rio de Janeiro a week later. We saw much of Rio, including a nightclub show with scantily dressed women. Ed was wide-eyed. We visited Paratay and had a schooner cruise – and then flew to Iguassu Falls. The falls were spectacular and bigger than Niagara Falls. We took a boat ride under the falls, which gave us a chance to see rainbows through the water. Our trip also included eating in an Argentine barbeque with many kinds of meat – really delicious.

We reached Las Campinas and stayed in a camp outside of town. We ate breakfast in Sao Paolo before going to the university. For some reason, no mention was made of where to get food, and no lunch was served. We thought we'd get a good meal at night, but all that was provided was a glass of wine and a small piece of bread with about a tablespoon of spread. Ed was starving. I told one of the students to take him to the kitchen and find something for him to eat. Chuck and I hoped we could find something to eat, but we didn't.

We left the main university about 10 p.m. with a group of Argentines. We were told we weren't to get off the bus. A little way out, the Argentines spotted a restaurant, so they got off and had a meal. We stupidly stayed on the bus. The group was in the restaurant for about an hour. There was no heat on the bus. We headed out, and as we went under a bridge, the bus got stuck. We all had to exit the bus while the driver eased it out. The next thing that happened was that we came to a railroad crossing and the gate was down with a small locomotive parked nearby. We waited and waited, but the locomotive didn't move, and the gate stayed down. It was getting later and later, and we were all freezing. Finally, the student who had come with us got out of the bus, raised the gate, and we passed by the locomotive. We continued on. We came to a turn on the road near where we were supposed to stay, and just as we started to turn, there was a noise, and the bus jerked to a halt. The student lost her footing and slid down the aisle. The driver and the student got out to look. The tie bar at the front of the bus was broken. We had stopped about three feet short of a 15 or 20-foot deep hole in the road. We all felt a guardian angel was with us that night.

After an hour or so, and a call for help, another bus came and took us to our camp. It was 3:30 a.m., and we were supposed to be picked up for the conference at 7 a.m. We had a roll and coffee for breakfast. The camp was primitive, and after our night's adventure, we decided to stay at a hotel in town. What a happy decision!

October found us on a cruise to the Caribbean, where we visited St. Kitts, St. Martin, St. Croix, Puerto Rico, St. Barts, Antigua, Barbados, Martinique, Grenada, and St. John. We enjoyed sightseeing and snorkeling.

After returning from our trip, Chuck had hernia surgery on an outpatient basis. He had learned about medical uses of hypnosis at the Milton Erickson Institute in Arizona. He was eager to see whether he could use self-hypnosis instead of traditional anesthesia. The anesthesiologist agreed, as long as he could stand by. Chuck needed no regular anesthesia, had the operation, came home, and ate his breakfast. At home, he realized his right foot felt cold but was warm when he touched it. He had told his right foot to be cold instead of feeling any pain. His hypnotic suggestion had worked. He also told his body it would be healed in a week or two, and it was healed. When other patients would ask that doctor how long it would take for them to heal, he'd respond, "I had one crazy psychologist who recovered in less than two weeks."

1995

Chuck and I had offered to do counseling workshops for the American Counseling Association. In January, were invited to go to the Virgin Islands and put on workshops on the islands of St. Croix and St. John. We stayed in the homes of members of the association and enjoyed their hospitality. One member grew anthuriums in his greenhouse. They were on display in his home. The flowers were three inches across, and the stems must have been three to four feet long. I had never seen such big ones.

After returning from the island, Chuck had throat surgery to help offset his sleep apnea. He did well. This time the anesthesiologist wouldn't let him use his hypnosis. About two weeks after the surgery, we flew to Rome and rented a car for two weeks. We drove through Italy and Sicily, marveling at the Greek and Roman ruins. Sicily was especially interesting. In Agrigenta, a Roman villa has been found containing colorful mosaic floors. I was astonished to see mosaics of black and white people shown along with many types of animals.

In the catacombs of a church in Palermo, there are mummies of people who died in the eighteenth century. The bodies have ropes around their necks and are hung on pegs in the walls. Children are grouped together, as are priests, women, and men. A soldier was in a casket with a tri-corner hat laying upon his breast. The female children wore bonnets, gloves, and white leather shoes, as well as beautiful dresses. I was so intrigued with the costumes that I didn't feel uncomfortable seeing the bodies.

In Siracusa, we saw a huge crowd walking on a promenade beside the water. It was late afternoon, and the sun was about to set. We thought it might be a holiday and asked if this were so. We got a strange look from the person, who said, "No, we're just watching the sun go down." We should have known, but where at home would we have seen a crowd watching the sunset? We returned to Rome, turned in the rental car, and flew home.

Late June saw us again flying to Europe, but this time, we flew to England and rented a car. We had found a club that people could join and get the names of teachers who wanted to swap houses. We had contacted four families in England and Wales, and they agreed to keep the four of us (Ed and Candace were with us). We got to visit different parts of England and learn about British life. I am still in contact with three of these families.

Some school children in England have a unique way to learn about their history. Once a year, a manor house's grounds are open for groups of teachers and children to go and stay a week. A year in history is chosen to be re-created. When we visited, the year was 1580. The children and teachers had to speak Elizabethan English. They learned to play instruments of that time, to dress accordingly, and to eat foods that the people of that time would have eaten, using utensils of that period. They raised ferrets as pets, which we were allowed to hold. As we watched, a ferret escaped from a woman's hands and dashed inside her blouse!

Our international conference this summer was in Dundee, Scotland. We left our new British friends and went to Scotland. We visited Edinburgh and Loch Ness. We were disappointed to not see the monster.

We returned home to our regular activities and waited until September to travel once more. If Chuck had had his way, we would have been home a month and travelled a month.

In late September, we took a military hop to Rota, Spain. We then took a bus to Sevilla, and from there, flew to the island of Menorca by way of Mallorca. The Parkers, whom we had met when we took our trip to the Galapagos Islands, had a home on Menorca, and they had invited us to visit. Their home was built on the edge of a cliff and into the cliff, overlooking the water. One could watch the ships come and go. The water was a beautiful blue. We visited the entire island as well as the island of Mallorca. Since our friends were soon emigrating to Australia, we were fortunate to be able to visit the beautiful islands. We hated to say "good-bye," but we had to return home.

1996

Thinking back, this year and the following years were the ones when we seemed to really be on the go. Early in the year, we flew to Puerto Rico and spent a week. We returned and drove to Pittsburgh to attend the American Counseling Association Annual Convention. One evening, we went to a reception held at Duquesne University. We left the university after midnight to go back to our motel. We had to pass through a very poor neighborhood known for its high crime rate. As we drove through, our car suddenly stopped and wouldn't start again. We pushed it to the curb. We saw a lighted gas station about half a block away. Chuck told me to stay in the car and lock the doors. He would go to the garage. When he reached the garage, the customers realized we weren't from their neighborhood. They asked if he were alone. When he said he wasn't, they told him to get me and bring me to the garage. The AAA man was called. As more customers came, they offered to help in any way they could and then stayed to guard us. By the time the tow truck arrived, over an hour later, quite a crowd had gathered. We realized that any neighborhood has caring people.

In June, Ed, Candace, Chuck, and I flew to Europe, this time to Paris. We visited our friends in Orleans and

Bourges and then traveled along the Loire River to see the various castles. We visited Angers where my father-in-law had been in World War I. A French farmer there had wanted Chuck's dad to marry his daughter.

We paid a visit to a family in Auxerre before our teacher swap with a family in Lyon and Marignier (which is in the Alps). In the latter city, we stayed in a chateau built in 1787. Our custom was to ask our host to plan day trips to see interesting things in the area. We left Marignier and took the Mont Blanc tunnel to Turin, Italy, where we saw the famed Shroud of Turin. Our last teacher swap was in Brouchotte near the Alsace region. We visited Albert Schweitzer's home there.

During our trip, we passed through Clermont-Ferrand, which has ties to Greenville, my city. We tried to find a place to park our car, but all the lots were full. We finally saw a sign that said "parking." We didn't notice that it also said "weekends only." We saw a car going into the garage and followed. The gates closed behind us. We were in a garage beneath a large office building. We realized we had made a mistake, but we didn't know how to get out. We finally saw the woman whom we had followed and explained our plight. She called security and they helped us leave, but not before scolding us.

We drove to Germany and visited Aachen, where Charlemagne was crowned in 800 A.D. Then we went to Bonn where we saw Beethoven's birthplace and Konrad Adenauer's home. Ed was taking piano lessons at this time and enjoyed playing on Schumann's piano and a piano similar to one used by Chopin. We bought him sheet music composed by both musicians at his request. A friend, Erika, in Göttingen had asked us to come visit her. She and Ed enjoyed playing a duet together; she played the flute, and he played the viola.

We left Germany and again visited our friends, the Stansliks, in Poland. Along the way, we saw large trucks carrying car parts. They were being shipped to Russia where they would be reassembled and sold. Apparently, there was a great need for cars in Russia, as many cars were stolen in the Eastern Bloc countries and taken there. Our friends had swapped their small apartment for a larger one in a house built during the early 1930s. They insisted that we stay with them. The bathroom was a disaster. The tub was old and rusted, and the toilet had a knob on the top which one pulled to flush. Each time the parts in the tank came out, and we had to then put them back in to be ready for the next flush.

The kitchen wasn't in much better shape. There was a stove, but the oven didn't work and neither did all the top burners. Before we left, we said we wanted to buy something for the family. It was suggested that we purchase wine glasses. We said we had something else in mind. We insisted Joanna go with us to buy a new stove since she, and not her husband, would be the one using it. She suggested originally that her husband could go and choose one. We made sure the stove was delivered while we were there. When we left Poland, we still had some Polish currency that we found we couldn't convert outside of Poland. I took a chance and sent the money (from the U.S.) to our friends. They received it and used it to buy a dishwasher.

After leaving Piła, we drove through Posnan, Wroclaw, and Krakow to Banska Bystrica to visit the family of Michel, the student we had met previously. Families there add a new story to their houses, as it is needed for each generation. When we arrived we found that there were nine of us in Michel's home. Michel's parents moved in with the grandparents on a different floor.

Candace liked to wash her long hair every night. I told her that would be impossible there with all these people and only one bathroom. I later realized the bathroom was also used to wash clothes, and I saw sheets being washed in the bathtub.

Banska Bystrica was the site of mass executions during World War II. Michel's grandmother had lived under both Nazi and Communist rule. She was all bent over from heavy work. I thought she must be 90, but she turned out to be younger than I.

With the family, we visited the Tatra Mountains (noted for winter skiing) and many other points of interest. Slovakia has some beautiful scenery and is a great vacation spot. It is less industrial than the Czech Republic.

We left our friends and journeyed on to Eger, Hungary, where our international school psychologists' meeting was held. Eger is an old city with a baroque university. The cathedral sits on a hill opposite the university. Each day at noon, there was an organ concert, which we enjoyed.

The university housed an interesting museum. The item that fascinated me the most was a clock built in England in the 1700s. It was a small cannon, less than nine inches long, with a place where gunpowder could be stored. There was a mirror, which reflected light on the gunpowder when the sun shone on it. The cannon was placed in the sun, and at exactly twelve o'clock noon, the sun would be reflected, and the heat would make the powder explode. The owner of the clock would then know it was noon (perhaps time to eat). After the end of the conference, we drove through Munich to Paris and flew home.

1997

We had now been married 50 years. We celebrated with a drop-in at our church to which many of our friends were invited. Mother was there in a wheelchair. Her health was declining, as she was now over 90 years old. She had been hospitalized with ulcers during the year. Because of her health, we decided not to attend the psychologists' meeting, which was held in Australia.

In August, we decided we'd fly to Rota, Spain. Our friends from Menorca put their car on the ferry, landed in Barcelona, and drove to Rota to meet us. We had prearranged with Tom to go to the travel agent just outside the back gate of the naval base and let her know where they were staying. Together, we explored Portugal. We stopped at Ponta de Sagres to see Henry the Navigator's school. In Evora, we visited the church of St. Francis and saw the bones of 5000 monks. At Fatima, we watched as pilgrims on their knees made their way to the altar. One lady's knees were bleeding. In Coimbra, we visited the university with its library and chapel as well as the cathedral. We also visited Santiago de Compostela to see the crypt where the remains of St. John are in a silver reliquary.

After leaving Portugal, we crossed over to Spain and visited Trujillo. This was the region from which many of the Spanish explorers of the New World came. As we walked around the square, a woman approached us and asked us whether we would like her to tell us about her city. We agreed we would. She said the women of the city had given their gold jewelry to be used for artifacts in the cathedral. She then pointed to a large house and said: "One time a family lived there who had twins. They also had a pet monkey. One day the monkey grabbed one of the twins and carried him to the roof of the house. The parents were horrified, as they were afraid the monkey would throw the baby off the roof. The mother ran outside with the remaining baby and his bed and put him where the monkey could see him. She then put the bed of the baby who was with the monkey beside the other baby and called to the monkey to bring the baby down and put him in his bed. After some time, the monkey obeyed, and the baby was saved." She said we would probably have a hard time believing the story, but that it was a true tale told by her great grandfather.

Princess Diana's funeral took place at this time. We were near Seville, and we spent the morning in our hotel room watching the funeral on TV. The next day was our fiftieth wedding anniversary. We stopped at a supermarket and bought a chocolate cake, which turned out to be one of the best I have ever eaten. We celebrated at a restaurant with paella, a huge salad, and our cake. We planned to order more, but the waitress said she didn't think we would be able to eat more. She was correct. We left the restaurant, went back to the base and flew home! Our friends Tom and Connie then went back to Menorca.

Upon returning home, we drove to Williamsburg where we had spent part of our honeymoon and enjoyed reliving the past. I remembered having eaten at the Williamsburg Inn, where violin music accompanied our dinner. I don't recall whether this time we had music, but we did enjoy a fine meal.

We had both been active throughout the year with our professional activities, and I had set up the counseling convention, which took a lot of time and effort.

Alice and Chuck in the Caribbean

1998

We started our year with Canal Zone friends on a cruise to the Bahamas. We were home for a couple of months before going to Brussels. We visited friends in Belgium, Germany, and France. We visited many of the World War I sites in Belgium and France, including trenches used in the war.

In July, we flew to Warsaw and took the train to Poznan and then continued to Piła. Our friends greeted us and took us home. Their first words were: "You've got to see our new bathroom." The bath had been all done over and now included a corner shower. Chrome glistened on the mirror, shower, and all the fixtures. In addition, they had made over the kitchen with new cabinets and a sink. These complemented the stove and dishwasher we had given them on our last visit. They also had a telephone since Yarek was a doctor. One had to wait nine years for a phone at that time, unless it was required for his profession.

One weekend, we drove to Prague with the Stansliks. At the Czechoslovakian border was a shop that sold Czech glassware. I bought some vases and beads, which I enjoyed. When we reached Prague itself, we found a nice hotel. We left our baggage and went to get a streetcar to go to the center of the city. Chuck and the Stansliks got on the train.

As I started to get on, two men stood in the doorway to block my entrance. They were huge and appeared determined to keep me from getting on the train. I thought to myself that they were rude and realized I could slip under the arm of one of the men. Without much thought, I dashed underneath his arm and found my party. Chuck shouted, "Watch your purse, Alice!" The men exited the car. I then realized that they meant to rob me after separating me from my friends and Chuck. Chuck seemed to think the men were gypsies.

We were on our way to Riga, Latvia, for our annual summer conference and had planned to take the train from Warsaw to Latvia. However, there had been a flood, and the train tracks were washed out somewhere between the two countries. Instead, we took a ferry from Gdynia, Poland, to Karlskrona, Sweden. We spent the night there and then took the train to Stockholm. The Swedish trains were excellent. They seemed almost new. Electronic signs told passengers the next train stop, the time of the stop, and the distance.

When we reached Stockholm, we found every hotel was full due to a convention of gay people. An elderly lady who rented rooms came up to Chuck in the station and said she would take us to her home and keep us. We were grateful and accepted her offer. She gave us dinner and breakfast and then gave us a bag of grapes to feed us on our journey.

When we finally reached Latvia by ferry, we were completely confused about where to go. We knew we were to go to the Latvian Agricultural College, but we didn't know where it was. We asked several people and learned we had to take a train to get there. We rode to our destination, but when we got off the train, we found ourselves in a place with no houses or other buildings and no one to give us directions. We had to guess which way to walk. We had a long walk to the college with our bags, but we finally made it. Each night, we had to walk to the train station and take the train to Jurmala where there were restaurants. Often, it was raining and many times, my back ached. I wished there was some place closer to eat.

One thing that was lacking in Latvia at that time was restroom service. We learned when we went to Riga to stop at McDonald's, which had a clean restroom. On a trip to Estonia, we found only one stop, and that was a dirty privy. Later, when we returned to Warsaw, there were no stops between Riga and Vilnius.

Some of the people attending the conference had ties to Latvia. Maria's father (a German World War II soldier) had died in Latvia, and others of Jewish background had ancestors who lived there.

On one of our sightseeing trips, Chuck and I started talking to Israel, who was an Israeli. Chuck asked him about his family to see if they had come from Latvia. Israel told us his family came from a small village in Poland where there were many Jews. His father was a cavalry officer in the Polish army, which was unusual for a Jewish man. He had a large beautiful horse. During the Second World War, when the Germans were retreating and going back through Poland, the Jews were in danger. Israel's father realized this, left his post by horseback, and went to warn the villagers to flee to Russia. No one in the village heeded his warning, and they were later killed. Israel's father got his family together, hitched up a cart to the horse – and they headed to the Ural Mountains in Russia. Israel was nine months old at the time. How they got food or where they finally settled, I never learned. The Germans strafed the escaping refugees. The horse pulling the wagon bolted and ran away. They had to buy a smaller horse from someone along the way and put a blanket on the animal to make him fit the stanchions.

At some point, Israel's father was arrested and sent to prison. His mother kept the family together. A Jewish custom is that, at the end of the day, leftover change is put into a pot (called a piska), and when there is enough money, is it given to some charity. The mother asked at the local hospital if there was someone she could help. There was a young woman who had lost one leg when she fell under a train. Her name was Rachael. She had been on her way, with bread, to a prison where her husband was incarcerated. A thief had stolen her bread, and she had run after him to recover it. She slipped and fell under the train. Now, she was despondent and wanted to die.

Israel's mother took the money to her and then continued to visit her and encouraged her to live. Sometime later, Israel's father was released from prison and told the family to go back to their village in Poland, and he would meet them there. The family remained there about seven years before emigrating to Israel.

Sometime later, Israel's older brother came home and announced that he was going to get married to a wonderful girl. He said, "I have something to tell you: her mother has only one leg." His mother asked, "And would her name be Rachael?" It was!

We took the train back to Warsaw as soon as the train service was restored and flew back home.

Ed Latimer's graduation from Carnegie Mellon University

1999

Mother Latimer was now 97 years old. The first part of the year, she was in the hospital seven times with pneumonia.

In early June, Ed was to graduate from the California Academy of Math and Sciences. We wondered whether we should leave Mother. She encouraged us to go and felt we should be with Ed for his graduation. She died on the seventh day of June, just before our return. Mother's mind was active until the end. The night before she died, she had called out each family member's name and said she loved him. She was buried in the Lickville Presbyterian Church cemetery next to Dad.

Jim and his family flew to South Carolina for Mother's funeral. Shortly after, we all attended a family reunion and later joined the Power Squadron for a trip along the North Carolina coast. We visited New Bern, Bath, and Oriental. The trip had a sad ending when a guest of one of the Power Squadron members collapsed and died on one of the tour buses.

While we were in Los Angeles, Jim, Ed, and Richard had parts in the neighborhood church's presentation of "Fiddler on the Roof." They enjoyed working together, and we were happy to be there to see the play.

As a sign of our aging, we both had cataract surgery, with good success. I was surprised that the world no longer looked yellow as it had before the surgery. In the spring, we had visits from our friend Henny from Turkey and her sister Renata from Germany. The Heffords also visited from England. This was the Heffords' second visit with us. During their first visit, their son was conceived.

We cancelled our usual European trip in the summer and instead spent time in Maine with our friends, the Bakers. We enjoyed eating lobster and sailing along the coast of Maine.

Ed was accepted into Carnegie Mellon University with an Air Force ROTC scholarship. He decided to major in computer science. He was excited to be able to take flying lessons. We met him in Atlanta in August and drove him to Pittsburgh.

I had spent the last year as president of the South Carolina Counseling Association, which kept me busy. I had also been appointed by the governor to serve on the Greenville County Disabilities and Special Needs Board. The board met monthly to oversee the operation of the organization for the handicapped.

Before the year ended, we took a relaxing cruise in the Caribbean on the Holland America ship, New Amsterdam.

During this year, Chuck had enjoyed being a member of the "Silver-Haired Legislature." This body made recommendations to the state legislature on issues affecting the elderly.

2000

As I have read over our travel notes and Christmas letters for the early part of the twenty-first century, I am amazed that we managed to see so much in so short a time.

At the close of December 1999, we flew to Brussels where we were met by Marc, our Belgian friend who had visited us earlier in Greenville. He and his wife had come to see what was being done for the mentally handicapped here. While visiting their home in Kortrijk, Belgium, we saw the facilities for the disabled there. I must say they are far ahead of us with their handling of these folks, especially the handicapped. Engineers have designed machines so that parts can be made for washing machines, cars, and other appliances. Contracts are made with large European companies, and money is brought in to make the workshops largely self-supporting.

While in Belgium, we visited many World War I sites, including Ypres, where there are arches with the names of 2000 British soldiers whose bodies were never identified. I saw the names Latimer and Whittaker and wondered if any of these people were related to us.

After four days in Belgium, we flew to Athens where we were to pick up our cruise ship. Athens had had the first snow in 10 years, and it was near freezing.

A German man, Karl, whom Chuck had met via the Internet, got us a hotel room and invited us to supper. The next day, we rented a car and drove to Evia, seeing snow-capped mountains along the way. We ate at a not too clean restaurant, and both of us were sick later. We subsequently returned to our hotel.

The next morning, we boarded our cruise ship on our way to South Africa. The first stop was at Malta, where we each took a different tour. I took the medieval tour where I went to the Inquisitor's Palace and visited a church and a museum.

Our next stop was La Goulette, Tunisia. We went to the Bardo Museum, which had formerly been a bey's palace. We drove to Carthage and saw Roman baths. The mosaics we saw were exquisite.

It had been raining as we travelled, but the sun appeared just as we reached Gibraltar, which enabled us to get a great view of the rock.

The next day we arrived at Casablanca. Another couple and we took a taxi ride to Rabat. It was a seven-hour drive. We saw beautiful big farms along the way.

In Rabat, we visited the mausoleum of King Mohammed, which was beautiful, especially the ceiling. At the Roman ruins, we saw about 300 storks, which had built six or eight nests per tree. The nests were huge. I called the area the "Stork Condos."

Our next stop was Senegal. The houses were pink and orange, and there were bougainvillea and baobab trees all around. Many slaves were shipped from there to the United

States and the Caribbean. One interesting place we saw was the Pink Lake. When the sun hit it, the water was orange, pink, and purple. Salt is taken from this lake and sent all over Africa. A large bag of salt cost one dollar. The women here wore colorful dresses and matching headpieces. We saw many carrying goods on their heads. Goats with kids walked along the roads.

After a day at sea, we reached Abidjan, Ivory Coast. With a couple from our ship, we visited the National Museum to see the exhibit of native arts – masks and sculptures. At the Bunco River, we watched people washing clothes. Each person had his own stone and space to wash. Clothes appeared to be scrubbed clean. We saw many palm trees, which are grown for their oil. Craftsmen make wicker and wooden furniture, as well as beautiful batik cloth.

Tema, Ghana, was our next stop. Traffic was terrible as we got off the ship, and it didn't appear to get any better until late in the day. After getting a taxi, we rode along a beautiful beach. We stopped at an attractive hotel on the beach. A clerk in the gift shop said I looked like Queen Elizabeth, who had recently visited there.

After our stop at the hotel, we drove to Accra to see the Nkruma Mausoleum and nearby museum. There were pictures of Nkrumah with several American Presidents. On the way back, we stopped at a shop to see coffins being made. There was a high window overlooking the street, displaying several types. The coffins were made of wood and paper mache. I was amazed to see coffins made to look like a cow, a fish, and a Mercedes Benz. I had once seen coffins similar to those in a museum in Rio de Janeiro.

Ghana appeared to be more westernized than the other African countries we had visited. The women weren't wearing the colorful dresses we had seen elsewhere. After leaving Ghana, our ship took us to Lome, Togo. Our first stop was at a hotel to change a 200-franc bill, which was worth $37.00. Chuck put the money in his pocket. A short time later, a man wanted to shine Chuck's shoes. He said "no." When we later went to the National Museum and Chuck was to pay the entrance fee, he found the money was no longer in his pocket. I suppose the shoeshine man had helped himself to it.

There is voodoo worship in Togo. We visited a fetish market (which appeared to be on a garbage dump) where we saw animal tails, desiccated and eviscerated birds, animal skins, skeletons, and parts of many other creatures. Whether or not these articles are used in their worship, I didn't find out. We did go to Togblekope to watch voodoo dancing and a voodoo ceremony. At the ceremony, we were seated while a band played and women danced. Several people went into a trance, fell to the ground, and writhed there covered in dust. A chicken was squeezed to death after two men tried unsuccessfully to strangle it from a distance by pulling a cord around a wooden chicken made from a stick.

Our next stop was Benin. We stopped at the port Cotonou. There, we got a taxi and had to pay for the gas, as the driver had no money. We had quite a wait at the gas station, as all motor scooters are served before cars. Our taxi took us to Porto Novo to see King Toffa's palace, which was made of adobe and had no furniture. A voodoo dance was being held in the courtyard. The dancers wore costumes that resembled haystacks. One had an airplane model on top. After the dance was over, the haystacks were removed. Under each haystack, we saw something different. Under one was a dancer. Under another was a goose, and another had two statues. We left and drove to Ganvie to Lake Nokoue. People were walking around on stilts. We visited a museum and an old colonial French home. Our next stop was in Ouidah, which is called the "voodoo capital." We were stopped en route by a man who threw a steel rod with spikes on the road and demanded money to remove the rod. Since we didn't want our tires punctured, the driver paid and we went on.

In Ouidah, we went to the temple of the sacred python. We saw twelve sleeping pythons. A guide said the pythons crawled into the city at night to eat mice and rats. The people did not have to feed them. If villagers found the snakes, they were brought back to the temple. Frankly, I'm glad we didn't have to pick up a python. The guide did insist that we each have our picture taken with a non-poisonous snake draped around our necks. He said we should do it to show our grandchildren that we weren't afraid of snakes. I tolerated the snake for the sake of the photo.

We were getting closer to South Africa. In late January, we stopped at Namibia, including Walvis Bay where we saw flamingos. We visited Swakopmund, which has beautiful houses. These are summer homes for wealthy Germans. A museum there holds the world's largest quartz crystal.

After a day at sea, we reached Luderitz, which was formerly a diamond-mining town, but was now a ghost town. A Norwegian ship was in the harbor dredging for diamonds. Sand from the Namib Desert had gotten into the abandoned buildings and had to be removed before the ghost town could be a tourist attraction. The large recreation center had been half full of sand. An old home that had belonged to Luderitz, founder of the town, was interesting because of the furniture and stained glass that it contained.

South Africa

Both of us were eager to visit South Africa because it had been in the news, and we were anxious to see what had happened since apartheid ended. When we landed at Cape Town, we were met by the De Jongs. Terry is a school psychologist who later emigrated to Australia. We picked up Maria Krull Buchholtz, our German friend, at her hotel, as she had arrived a few days earlier from Germany. We visited the waterfront and had tea in a restaurant along the wharf. There were beautiful condos and guesthouses along the bay. We went through Constantia and stopped at the De Groot winery to buy some wine.

A visit to Cape Town wouldn't have been complete without a visit to Robben Island, where Mandela had been a prisoner. Our guide had been a prisoner for five years himself. He spoke of the abuses, both physical and psychological, that they endured. Letters sent to prisoners were cut apart, censored, and the handwriting forged. Prisoners were made to feel that their families had abandoned them.

Following that visit, we took a taxi to the top of Table Mountain, where we saw lots of tiny animals (called dassies) and enjoyed a superb view. A dinner with the De Jong family included babotie (a South African meat casserole) and rooibos tea.

The next morning, Chuck drove our rented van to Cape Agulhas with stops at Hermosa and Elim. Here were white thatched roof cottages. At Cape Agulhas, we stayed at a bed and breakfast built in the 1920s that was owned by a former South African airline stewardess and Mensa member. Chuck also was a member of Mensa.

From there, we drove to Mossel and hence to Tsitsikamma National Park (Storm River) where we stayed in a cabin overlooking the ocean. We could hear the ocean's waves crashing all night.

We passed through the Tsitsikamma Reserve along the Garden Route to Port Elizabeth. We stayed at Avocet B&B, which was beautiful. Friends from the International School Psychology Group, the Kotzes, lived in Summerstrand on the edge of Port Elizabeth. Hans drove us about to see all the sights and we had braai (barbeque) at their home.

The following day, Hans drove us to Addo Elephant Park where there are hundreds of elephants. He parked the car near a water hole, and we sat for three-quarters of an hour while watching two mothers, two babies, and two adolescents. A baby would slide into the water, the mother would watch and then go to the edge of the hole--and with her trunk, push the baby out of the water. The baby would look around, look at his mother, and slide back into the water. This was repeated over and over. We watched with great amusement.

We left Port Elizabeth and drove through Bloemfontein, which was an attractive city with friendly people. We couldn't find a restaurant in the dark, but finally were escorted to one by two helpful policemen.

We had met a Bob Jones University student, Elaine Goodchild, who was from South Africa. She contacted her parents, who acted as our guides. They made all the reservations for our stopovers along the way, sometimes with relatives. We picked them up at their home near Johannesburg, and together, we first visited Clarence where a cousin of the Goodchilds lived. He showed us fields where bones of prehistoric animals had been found. From there, we went to Durban and visited friends from the International Psychology group. We went on to St. Lucia through Lesotho and to Kruger National Park. Unfortunately, there had been floods, and we weren't able to stay at the park as we had planned. Near Durban, we saw the place where Winston Churchill was captured during the Boer War.

We visited Pretoria and the Gold Reef historical mining park, as well as Swaziland. We went to Pilgrim's Rest and the Blyde River Canyon, both beautiful areas, before going to Kruger. Our accommodations were good throughout the trip. Some were cottages, and one was a grass hut similar to native huts enclosed in a high wire locked fence. At one place, we found monkeys climbing over the van and looking at themselves in the side mirrors.

We left the Goodchilds at their home and went to Mafikeng (formerly Mafeking) where there is a museum dedicated to Baden Powell, who founded the Boy Scout movement. We stayed at a park where there were lions and crocodiles. The windows in the dining room opened onto the ponds where the crocodiles lived. We watched them as we ate.

The park director gave us a tour of the park. He took us to where the lions roamed behind two wire fences. The lions growled at us, but our guide climbed between the fences and put his hand next to the fence closest to the lions. A big male came over, rubbing his head against the fence and the man's hand and purring loudly. You would have thought he was just a common house cat.

We stopped at a school run by German nuns, whom Maria knew, and then went to Kimberly to look into the deep hole from which diamonds were mined.

Our South African adventure really began when we were in the desert about 15 miles from Victoria West. We had been warned never to stop along the road in a deserted area. The van suddenly stopped because we were out of gas. The gas gauge showed that the tank was half full. Chuck said he'd flag down a car and that Maria and I should go to Victoria West for gas. He would stay with the van. He flagged down a car in which two white men were riding. Neither Maria nor I saw that they had guns strapped to their waists. The men agreed to take us to Victoria West but said we'd probably need to find a way back to the car. We got into their vehicle and Maria smiled and said, "You're such nice young men; I know you'll take care of us!" "Yes, we will. We're police officers," said one of the men. He was true to his word. They got gas for us, drove us back to the van, and made sure the van started before leaving us. They told us to stop at a well-known hotel, the Lord Milnes in Matjiesfontein, where we would be safe. We did so and had a fine night's sleep. We made it safely back to Cape

Town, and then flew back to Greenville at the end of February. We had been gone nearly three months, and Chuck had driven 6000 miles.

At the end of April, we were off again, but this time we flew to Los Angeles, Seoul, and Hong Kong. We visited Macau and then took a tour through the Pearl River Delta to Canton. I found that part of China to be beautiful, with parks, lakes, and temples. The farmers were prosperous. They raised ducks and fish to sell in the markets. We visited a shopping mall there that looked like any mall in the States. The people wore Western clothing and appeared stylish.

In Canton, we stayed at the White Swan Hotel, which is the most beautiful hotel I have ever seen. There were huge jade carvings in the lobby, some selling for over $1000.00. One carving was of a ship, another was a lion, and yet another was a mountain scene with trees and temples. We visited the market where we saw a huge barrel full of scorpions and another full of leeches. There were kittens and puppies in cages to be raised as food. The smell and sounds of the market will always be remembered. We had good meals, and I found China to be fascinating.

We returned to Hong Kong and boarded the Sky Princess for a cruise to Vancouver, British Columbia. Our first stop was Shanghai, China, where we visited temples and a music school. The children in the school gave us a concert. They were good. Instruction begins when the students are very young.

We then stopped at Pusan, Korea; Vladivostok, Russia; Hokkaido, Japan; Dutch Harbor, Aleutian Islands; and three ports in Alaska, and into Vancouver. In Vladivostok, we saw enormous new houses near the ocean that our guide told us belonged to drug barons. We saw whales and glaciers in Alaska. We spent a couple of days in Vancouver and then flew home.

We spent July in New England visiting friends and attending the annual School Psychology Colloquium. I carried a heavy corn stick pan to the conference to be transported back to South Africa for the Kotzes to use to make corn sticks. They had enjoyed this type of bread at our home.

Although we had been in Australia before, there were parts we hadn't seen. Tom and Connie had invited us to visit them near Brisbane. We had never been to Tasmania, nor to Adelaide, Ayers Rock, Alice Springs, or Darwin. We first visited Lina's family in Sydney and then went to Brisbane to see Tom and Connie, whom we had met on the Galapagos Islands trip. We had seen them earlier when they lived in Minorca. We then went to Newcastle to visit Vince Phelan and on to Darwin to see Anne Phelan.

Anne and Vince Phelan had visited us many years earlier when we lived in the Canal Zone. She had been a nun and he, a priest. They had left their orders, met as teachers, then married. They had been on an exchange program for teachers in Canada. They decided to drive through Central America before going back to Australia. Unfortunately, Vince contracted amoebic dysentery in Mexico, and by the time they reached Costa Rica, he was hemorrhaging and had lost 50 pounds. He was hospitalized. Anne knew no Spanish and was afraid to be alone.

Vince called us and we told him to put Anne on a bus to Panama. We would keep her until he was better. Anne came, and Vince arrived about a week later. They stayed with us about a month, until he regained his strength. They then flew back to Australia after selling their car. After several years together, they divorced, and both had found new companions.

When we visited Anne and her friend John in Darwin, she decided to take time off from working in her art shop and show us the area. There is a national park with primitive aboriginal drawings, as well as other interesting sights. The area around Darwin has areas where the aborigines live and outsiders are not welcomed. Anne is able to visit there as she buys their crafts for her art shop. We didn't get to visit these areas but did see the park and the area where our U.S. Air Force worked during World War II. One thing that fascinated me was seeing huge termite nests, some nearly three feet tall.

While we were in Tasmania, we got to see the Tasmanian devils that I had read about. These are small dark-haired animals with bad dispositions. Ayers Rock was beautiful both in the early morning and at sunset when it has a crimson glow. In Alice Springs, we wore our hats with veils because of the flies. While there, we celebrated Chuck's birthday with dinner and entertainment by their TV entertainer Ted Egan. Seeing Tom and Connie was a pleasure. We returned to Sydney and flew home.

At one of the school psychology meetings we had been asked to present workshops for the Baltic Psychology Conference. Some time later, we flew to Warsaw where

Maria met us. We used her car to drive us to Riga. We enjoyed a presentation of "La Traviata" at the National Latvian Theatre in Riga. We drove back to Warsaw through Lithuania, stopping to see Siaula's Hill of Crosses, as well as Thomas Mann's home. The hill of crosses represents crosses placed at a site by families who had family members killed by the Russians. At first the Russians took down the crosses, which were quickly replaced. The Russians finally allowed the crosses to stay. The crosses are made of wood, metal, stone or whatever the family could find to make them.

We stopped once again in Piła to see the Stansliks before heading home.

2001

For many years, we had wanted to visit Kenya. In January, the opportunity arose. We flew to Nairobi and stayed there for three days. Before we left Greenville, our minister told us he had a letter from a minister in Kenya asking for help in setting up a home for orphans of the AIDS epidemic. The minister wanted us to see if we could find out anything about this venture. In Nairobi, we found St. Andrews Presbyterian Church, which has 15,000 members and offers services in several languages. Since we were Presbyterians, we went there for information about the minister. Although the people of St. Andrews knew of the man, they didn't know what he was doing, and we decided to recommend that our church not support his project.

While we were at St. Andrews, the head minister asked where we planned to stay in Mombassa. We said we hadn't made any reservations and were planning to see what was available there. He said a member of his congregation owned a hotel, and he'd try to get us reservations there. He was as good as his word. The hotel was beautiful and full of people from northern Europe. It was on the beach. We stayed three days, and when we tried to pay, we were told we owed nothing. It was a gift.

While in Nairobi, we got a taxi and went to a game park where we saw many animals. We also went to a museum where they have a railroad car, which was used when the railroad was being built in Kenya. Apparently, there were many lions roaming about during that time and eating the workers. A man with a gun was put on a train by an open window so that he could kill any lion that might come along. Instead of his killing the lion, the lion killed him. Apparently, he fell asleep just as a lion came to the train. They showed us the car where the man had been killed. We took the sleeper to Mombassa. It reminded me of my train trip to California so many years ago. We had white-coated waiters in the dining car and the food was good and well served.

In Mombassa, we saw a workshop for the physically handicapped. Most of the clients had been ill with polio and were very handicapped. They didn't have the motorized equipment that we have for our people, which made it very hard for them to move around. There was a workshop where they made jewelry out of metal and stones, which they sell at shops around the world.

The sister of the hotel owner had started a home for orphans. The children ranged in age from two to eighteen years. I can't recall how many children were there, but I'd guess 30-40. The older ones cared for the younger ones. There were no screens on the building's windows, and malaria was ever present. The children were given malaria medicine, but some still got the disease. Our Navy left vitamin and mineral capsules each time they came into port, which helped the children. The children were fed rice and beans for breakfast, cornmeal and beans for lunch, and rice and beans for supper. The director hoped she could buy a cow to supply milk for the children. A shed had been built to house the cow whenever one could be obtained. I saw no store-bought toys of any kind for the children.

While we walked around, Chuck had one little boy on his shoulders and two clinging to his pants. I had three clinging to me. They didn't want to let go, and I knew they craved attention. I thought how lucky our children are because they have more than just the basic needs to survive.

We sailed on the Princess cruise line to India. We stopped at both the Seychelles and Maldives Islands. We found the Seychelles to be beautiful with a large botanical garden. In the Maldives, we visited the oldest mosque, dating back to 1656, and the National Museum.

Our first port in India was Cochin, where we took a drive around the city and watched the Kathakali dancers perform. Our next and final port was Bombay. On the dock, there was a large elephant adorned with flowers and gold trappings. We had arranged our visit with an Indian travel agency. We flew from Bombay to Madurai where we spent two nights at the Madurai Park Inn. We got a rickshaw to see the sights of the city, which included the Gandhi Museum and the Meenakashi Temple. We then flew to Chennai where we visited the Government Museum, the San Thome Basilica, and St. Thomas Mount where St. Thomas was supposed to have lived and preached. We also took a rickshaw and went to Mahabalipuram to view the sculptures made in the eighth century. We stayed at the YWCA in both cities. We flew to Delhi.

We had arranged for a car to pick us up and take us on the rest of our tour. The driver took us first to Jaipur, where we visited Jantar Mantar (the largest stone observatory in the world) and the Amber Fort, built in 1592. We had an elephant ride. Our driver then drove us to Agra to see the Taj Mahal. We stopped to visit a palace compound (Fatehpur Sikri) en route.

The Taj Mahal, built by Shah Jehan, was beautiful and I enjoyed seeing it. Times had changed since Chuck had last been there. I had to pay over $20.00 to stand in line and then go through only certain parts of the tomb. Chuck had gone when there was no fee, and one could wander all about. The natives paid in rupees what I had to pay in dollars. We also went to the Ayra Port and Itimad-ud-Daulah (a marble tomb built between 1622 and 1628 for Emperor Jahangir's Chief Minister). We saw many monkeys, and one of the creatures had climbed six floors to look in our window at our hotel in Agra. We also saw them climbing about inside several temples. The day we were in Delhi, before we had a driver, we went to the Red Fort, the Delhi Gate, the Craft Museum, and a beautiful garden where Gandhi's son is buried. While we were at the garden, an Asian couple came to me and wanted to each have a picture taken with me. I never figured out whether it was my white hair that attracted them or something else.

I left India with many different impressions. The cities are very overcrowded, which means people are always close to you. There seemed to be no zoning, and there were beautiful buildings in slum areas. There appeared to be few parks or gardens, and one could see pink, green, and white plastic bags blowing around in dusty lots. Hawkers bothered us wherever we went, either to sell us something or to get us to ride in their rickshaws. Barbers were shaving men along the street; food and goods were sold, and shoes were shined.

The artwork in India, on the other hand, is magnificent. Jewelry and carpets are very well made. The temples and tombs were beautiful with intricate inlays of semi-precious stones. India has an historical past with many different influences on its culture. It was wonderful to see such creativity amid all that squalor.

Chuck had been to India many years before on a State Department tour. Before leaving, we went to the Hotel Vikram in the Defense Colony in Delhi. Two of the employees remembered him after all those years. He had stayed for three months during his previous time there.

Alice and Chuck in Bangkok with grandson Richard
and Maria Krull Buchholz

ANGKOR WAT AND CAMBODIA

Three months after returning home from India, we joined 14 people on an overseas adventure tour of Thailand, Cambodia, Laos, and Vietnam. We flew from the United States one afternoon and reached Bangkok about 9 p.m. the next day. We were met by Anya, our guide. We spent the night in Bangkok and the next afternoon flew to Siem Reap, Cambodia. While there, we travelled by trishaw (a type of bicycle) with a sidecar.

Our purpose was to see Angkor, a holy city. The city covers six by sixteen miles and took centuries to build. It was constructed between 800 and 1200 A.D. by the Khmer aristocrats, who were either Hindu or Buddhist. It was 100 degrees the day we visited, but the heat didn't stop us from seeing the bas-reliefs at Bayon, Baphoun, and the Elephant's Terrace, the Terrace of the Leper King and Ta Prohm. We visited the aforementioned in the morning, and in the afternoon, we visited Angkor Wat (main temple) to wait for sunset to see it in all its glory.

Angkor Wat was built between 1113 A.D. and 1150 A.D. It is a large pyramid temple with a great moat surrounding it. Its towers are supposed to represent the center of the universe.

Before leaving Siem Reap, we had a boat ride on Tonle Lake, where the river people live. We saw thatched-roof houses on hollow bamboo poles, small markets, a post office, and a beauty shop—all floating on the water. This area fascinated me.

Our next stop was the Killing Fields Memorial Temple built near Phnom Penh to commemorate the deaths of

1.7 million victims of the genocide perpetrated by Pol Pot during 1975-1979. Phnom Penh was one of many execution sites in Cambodia. It is hard to imagine the cruelty that must have taken place.

We flew back to Thailand to commence our visit to that country. We had seen some beautiful countryside and fascinating sights.

A market in Vietnam

Thailand, Laos, And Vietnam

After returning to Bangkok, we saw the Grand Palace of Thailand, which was beautiful. It was decorated with broken china and colored mirrors. We wore the jasmine leis we had received the day before. I was interested in the palace because a member of the royal family had attended Simmons College (my alma mater) while her husband – later the king – attended Harvard University. After leaving the palace, we went to the flower market to see a wonderful array of blossoms.

The next day, before breakfast, we went to the Marble Temple to watch the local people bring food to the monks. We handed out juice and dried fish. After breakfast, we went down the river and along the canals on a long-tailed boat to a house that was 100 years old. There, we watched a cooking demonstration of chicken curry, which we ate for lunch. On the way back to the hotel, we visited the Temple of the Dawn and had planned to see the Royal Barges Museum, but it was closed because it was the Thai New Year. Because of the holiday, we were squirted with water, had white color painted on our faces, and had scented water poured over our hands.

The following day found us in Kanchanaburi and our lodge on the bank of the River Kwai. This area was where

12,300 Allied POWs and Asian conscripts died while they were forced to build the WWII railway. The film "The Bridge on the River Kwai" recounts that story. We walked on a part of the original bridge. We visited the War Cemetery and the Jeath Museum, constructed to look like the prisoner-of-war camp. There were mementos and pictures drawn by the captives. What a terrible life these prisoners must have had!

We stayed overnight there, and the next morning took a boat to Hell Fiore Pass where the Australian government has set up a museum. This area was one of the most difficult sections of the railroad to build. We left and took a train to Takilen Station.

Early the next day, we drove to Supanbure Bird Sanctuary through rice-growing country. We stopped at Utaithani to visit a local market. We cruised for two hours on a wooden rice barge, where we had our lunch. In the afternoon, we visited Wat Chantaram, a beautiful white temple.

There are historic ruins at Sukothai, where the Thai nation was born. The columns, shrines, temples, and palaces are well preserved. We visited them next. King Ramkhamhaeng lived here. He invented the Thai script, developed relations with China, and was skilled with hand-to-hand combat on elephant-back.

We continued to Chiang Rai where Burma, Laos, and Thailand meet. We had a boat ride on the Mekong River and briefly visited Laos.

We were supposed to visit Myanmar (also known as Burma), but there had been fighting on the border and we weren't allowed to go. We did walk to the middle of a bridge leading to Myanmar but were told not to go beyond a certain line.

While we were in Chiang Rai, we went to Mae Chan and got on trucks to go up the narrow mountain road to Mae Salong where the hill tribe people live. We visited the Yao tribe and the Ekaw tribe. Both have elaborate customs. That evening, we each had a Thai massage, which entailed a lot of pummeling. We visited the Mae Ping Elephant camp the next day and rode by elephant to another village and then back to Chiang Mai where we boarded a bamboo raft to go back downstream. The elephant we rode ate an entire stalk of bananas while we were riding on his back.

The last day in Chiang Mai, we visited Wat Chedi Luang and heard a lecture about Buddhism. We also visited Wat Phrathat Doi Suthep, another magnificent temple.

We returned to Bangkok by plane and had time to

An elephant ride in Mae Ping Village, Thailand

visit Wat Po, a monastery, which houses the largest reclining Buddha in Thailand. After dinner we watched a dance performance and then prepared to fly to Vietnam.

We visited Bat Trang Village, where pottery has been made for centuries. At the factory, roof tiles, as well as dining utensils, were being manufactured. The pottery was blue and white.

We drove to Ha Long Bay via rough roads dotted with rice paddies and small villages. We had a day's cruise on a wooden sailboat. The Gulf of Tonkin, on which we were sailing, has over 3000 islands composed of carboniferous chalk and covered with vegetation. The islands are of different sizes and shapes. Two facing islands look like the heads of a man and a woman. Our guide, when we saw these, said, "May I ask you a question?"

I replied, "Yes, you may."

She said, "Your man, he is so big, and you are so small. How does he *keeese* you?"

I told her we'd show her, and we did. She also liked my white hair and kept patting my head while saying, "So pretty, so soft."

We returned to Hanoi, did a bit more sightseeing, and flew home. Everyone was kind and thoughtful, and one would never have thought that quite a few years earlier we had been at war with them. Dollars were the money of choice there.

Summer In Europe

In early June, we flew to Brussels and again visited our friends in Kortrijick. From there, we took the TGV train to Paris. Richard and Lauren were with us. We spent a week there seeing the sights of Paris. Richard and Lauren stayed with a French family, and we stayed at a small hotel. The lady in whose home Richard and Lauren stayed was a teacher. She came home for lunch but then went back to school until late afternoon. Meals at night, therefore, were served around 8 p.m.

One morning, we went to a launderette to wash our clothes. A nicely dressed young man came in and chatted with Chuck while he washed his clothes. When we were finished and the man had gone, Chuck realized his camera was missing. He had had it attached to his belt.

We left Paris, rented a car, and took the Chunnel to England. When we reached England, we spent time visiting our friends in Colchester, Bradford-on-Avon, and Stotfold. After our visit there, we took the ferry from Portsmouth to St. Malo in France. Since Lauren and Richard hadn't been in France, we took them to Normandy to see Omaha Beach and the Bayeau Tapestries. We stayed at French farms, which are like our bed and breakfasts. On one farm, we arrived while the farmer was milking. Richard or Lauren was handed a pitcher of warm milk for us to use. One of them remarked, "We have real milk."

We drove to Bourge and visited our friends there and then spent a week driving through the Loire Valley, stopping to see many of the chateaus. We found the architecture of the chateaus to be most beautiful; many were truly opulent. We left the valley and went to Dinan where the International School Psychology Colloquium was being held. Chuck conducted a workshop at the meeting. After the conference ended, we drove to the Isle of Jersey where we watched a medieval reenactment complete with falcons. Lauren and Richard were fascinated. Afterward, we returned to Brussells and flew home.

In the late summer, Tom and Connie came from Australia to visit us. We had visited them in Menorca and in Australia. We drove them up the East Coast, stopping in Williamsburg and Washington en route. When we

Australian friends, Tom and Connie, who were with the Latimers for their fiftieth wedding anniversary in Spain and their sixtieth in England

reached New Jersey, I joined my high school class for our sixtieth reunion, Tom and Connie visited friends, and Chuck went to New York to see the rubble left from the bombing of the World Trade Center.

After the close of my reunion, we drove our friends up to New England where we all stayed at a cottage in Maine owned by people we had met on our trip to the Galapagos Islands. We were there a month.

We returned home to resume our professional, social, and community activities. It had been quite a year of travel, and we were glad our health still permitted it.

2002

After the 9/11 disaster, airport security became more stringent, and security staff were not trained to work with the mentally handicapped. When we had taken Mary with us to California in December of 2001, the security person on duty took Mary's pen and notebook from her and spoke sharply to her, causing her to get angry and hit me. As a result, the security agent wasn't going to let us on the plane. She said that Mary might attack the passengers. An airline supervisor saw what was going on and told security he'd take over. He put us on the plane ahead of everyone else and got Mary calmed down. As a result of this incident, we determined we wouldn't have Mary fly again. If we were to go to California again for Christmas, we would leave Christmas Day after spending Christmas Eve with Mary.

In January, we had a visit from Charles and April Fawcett who were on their way back to London from Los Angeles. Charles (now deceased) was a cousin of Chuck's. He helped smuggle thousands of people out of France during World War II. Later, he became an RAF pilot and served in the French Foreign Legion. He became a movie actor in Italy and later helped the Afghans against the Soviet Union's invasion. When Charles died a couple of years ago, part of his ashes were placed here in Greenville. The rest of the ashes were left in Paris near where he had lived.

Ed completed his bachelors degree at Carnegie Mellon in three years. His degree was in computer science. He persuaded the Air Force to let him stay and get his masters degree. He was accepted for graduate school in Robotics. We joined Jim, Lina, and Richard in Pittsburgh for Ed's graduation in May. After the ceremony, we travelled together to Antietam, Harper's Ferry, Arlington, and Williamsburg. We had enjoyed quite a family get together.

In June, our German friend, Maria, met us in Los Angeles. From there, Maria, Chuck, Richard, and I flew to Taiwan, where we spent a week visiting the Chans whom we had visited earlier. They showed us places we had not visited before. Our next stop was Manila for the meeting of the International Council of Psychologists and the Philippine Annual Counseling meeting. Chuck made presentations at both meetings.

We were in Manila when there was a typhoon. Water in the streets was nearly up to the top of car tires. Fortunately, the first few days we were there were clear, and we got to visit some of the countryside. We ate at a restaurant where we had tiny French-fried crabs served on banana leaves. The crabs were delicious – we ate the claws and all.

Dr. Lily Rosqueta-Rosales hosted us for lunch one day. She was a neighbor of the president of the Philippines. She told us stories of the cruelty on the part of the Japanese during the Second World War. A Japanese officer went to her church. One Sunday, he told her family to flee to the woods and hide and not return home because the Japanese wanted to capture them. He would let someone know where they were to provide food for them. They followed his instructions. They never saw him again and presumed he had been killed for allowing them to escape. Later, they found their maid had been decapitated.

We had wanted to go to Corregidor. Because of the typhoon, it was uncertain if there would be a boat going to the island. When we checked, we were told there would be one going. One of the school counselors accompanied us. The crossing was extremely rough, and Richard was seasick all the way. When we reached Corregidor, the rain was coming from all directions. The counselor took us to a small hotel where we bought clean clothes for Richard, and he was able to get a shower and change. We were rain-soaked all day but were happy we were able to see where the fighting had taken place in World War II.

We left Manila and flew to Kuala Lumpur, Singapore, and Bangkok. Lina's sister-in-law was visiting her family in Singapore. We were invited to a delicious Chinese dinner, which we all enjoyed. In Bangkok, Maria purchased some new clothes. We were amazed at how quickly clothes could be made. She had her measurements taken in one day. The next day, she was fitted to a garment already sewed together. The third day, the finished garment was delivered to her room, packed in a plastic bag, and ready to be put in her luggage.

After leaving Bangkok, we flew to Munich. The school psychology meeting was being held in Nyborg, Denmark. Chuck used Maria's car to drive us all to Denmark. At the close of the meeting, we all went to Copenhagen and visited Tivoli's Garden. We then went to Sweden where we spent the night. We continued on to Oslo to see Kon-tiki and some Viking boats. We returned to Copenhagen by overnight ferry. We drove Maria back to her home in Wangen and flew home from Munich.

Back home in October, we joined the Power Squadron for a fall cruise on the Tennessee River and then drove to Florida to visit friends. We had had another wonderful year of travel.

2003

We spent Christmas of 2002 with Jim and Lina in California. After our visit with them, we had a brief cruise to Ensenada, Mexico. After returning home, we continued doing our community work, including church, the counseling association, and the Silver Haired Legislators, of which Chuck was a member.

March found us again in California to attend the American Counseling Association annual meeting. Following this, we took a two-week cruise from Hawaii to the Republic of Kiribasi (Fanning Island).

Our summer trip to China was cancelled due to the SARS epidemic. We did, however, go to Florida where we attended the Panama Canal Reunion and saw old friends.

The European branch of the Counseling Association was held in Willingen, Germany, during October. We attended the meeting and then drove to Northern Germany where we had spent many happy hours. Chuck had founded this counseling branch when we lived in Karlsruhe.

We stopped to see the school where Herr Kaspersmeier (Henny's father) had been the principal. Nearby, a couple was working in their yard, and we stopped to talk with them. They remembered Renata and Henny.

Jean and John Baker were to attend a gathering of John's West Point classmates at the Mission Inn in Ontario, California. The gathering was scheduled for November, and we were invited. The hotel is famous because many movie stars stayed there, and I think Jack Kennedy did as well. It is an interesting place to stay. We returned home and shortly thereafter drove to Pittsburgh where Ed received his master's degree and his commission as a second lieutenant in the Air Force. Ed had asked his grandfather, a retired naval officer, to administer the oath of office. Chuck was delighted to do this. Jim, Lina, and Richard were also with us. A big dinner had been planned for the evening after the ceremony with 18 people asked to attend. Several of Ed's friends had come from California to be with him.

Chuck started to read the oath when he saw that part of the page was black. Fortunately, he knew the oath and was able to continue. We did not realize anything was wrong. He had had a TIA, a precursor to a stroke. He should have told us and gone to a hospital immediately. He didn't want to spoil the dinner party so he said nothing until about 10 p.m. when he told Jim he'd have to drive to the airport the next day. We called our doctor in Greenville, who diagnosed a TIA. He said that Chuck should see a physician. Chuck, however, knew that they would hospitalize him, and he wanted to get home since it was almost Christmas. We returned home the next day, but it was too late to do anything. He lost some of the vision in his eyes and had become dyslexic. He could no longer be a speed-reader, but he could still type. We spent Christmas at home. In late December I celebrated my eightieth birthday with a large family party. Although my birthday is in September, no one could come then.

2004

After having the TIA, Chuck decided to resign from his many activities because he felt he couldn't give the same amount of attention to them as he had before. He decided to spend his time doing genealogy because he could get the information and then type it into the computer. He felt typing would help his reading. He found he couldn't look at a word and recognize it. He had to read it letter by letter.

He still enjoyed travelling, and in February, we took a cruise to Grand Cayman, Mexico, Aruba, Costa Rica, and Panama. We got off the ship in Panama and visited our old home, the places we had worked, and the areas now taken over by Panama. We were surprised to see on the Panama Canal four-family houses now done over as one large mansion. A lot of money has been put into the houses.

In April, Chuck had a severe stroke, which caused him to lose his right visual perceptive field. Although I'm sure he often got frustrated, he never complained and continued with his typing. Because it was hard for him to read, I read him the paper and whatever else he wanted me to read.

The school psychology group was meeting this year at the University of Exeter in England. Chuck was able to drive with me as navigator to read the signs. He drove

8000 kilometers with no difficulty. Jim, Lina, and Richard joined us in England, where we visited friends near London, East Anglia, and Wales. While we were in Dover at a museum, I noticed I couldn't see a picture in my camera when I used my right eye but could see it with my left. I had lost the central vision due to wet macular degeneration. I went first to the Navy Clinic in London, then to the Lakenheath Air Force hospital, and lastly to Cambridge University Hospital. At the latter, I met with a retinologist who told me to go home and have my eye treated. I followed his advice and found a retinologist at my own eye clinic in Greenville who treated me.

The trip to the English hospital was interesting. While I waited the first day to see the doctor, a man came in with a suitcase of dried fish (kippers) for one of the doctors. I was then seen in a ward with patients being admitted for surgery. The second day, while we waited, a young lady in uniform pushing a cart came in and took orders for the patients' suppers. When she had taken all their orders, she came and asked if Chuck and I would like some tea. We said, "yes" and enjoyed our tea while we waited. I've never had tea served at a hospital in the States.

We returned to Europe in October. We had invited Ed and Dot, Chuck's brother and sister-in-law, to meet us in Frankfurt and travel with us. We showed them Berlin and then went to Poland where we stayed at the inn in Piła. There was a wedding reception at the inn, which gave us something interesting to witness. We visited the Stansliks, and Ed kept Julia laughing by playing a game with her using his handkerchief. We went to Göettingen and visited with Erika. On the way, we spent the night at a mini hotel in Poland. We discovered that most of the foreign contractors helping with Polish infrastructure stayed there. The buffet breakfast served was more than I have ever seen served anywhere. Everyone was encouraged to take along food for midday as well. We continued on to Wangen to visit Maria and then flew to Lisbon to begin our cruise to Miami on the cruise ship Regatta. On returning home, we learned the Stansliks were divorced and Yarik had left the family and gone to Ireland. We felt sad.

Richard became an Eagle Scout just as Ed had done several years before. Ed completed his UPT (Undergraduate Pilot Training) and enjoyed flying. We looked forward to seeing him get his wings.

2005

An ice storm at the end of December 2004 knocked out our power for five days. After spending one day at home, we gladly accepted an invitation to stay with our friends, the Hiltons. Chuck's health appeared to be better. He recovered most of his visual field except for blurring in the upper right corner. He still swapped letters and numbers and read word by word instead of paragraph by paragraph.

Most of the winter was spent in Greenville while we enjoyed activities at our church (St. Giles Presbyterian) as well as our other civic and social obligations. Mary had chosen our church when we first arrived in Greenville. It was May, and there was a picnic on the lawn. She said, "I want to go there."

With the coming of spring in March, we drove to Florida and took a cruise with the Power Squadron from Tarpon Springs to Sarasota. In June, we drove to Boston for my sixtieth reunion at Simmons College. After the close of the reunion, we drove to Cape Cod to visit Helen, a childhood friend, and Frances, a college friend. We enjoyed Cape Cod and its delicious seafood.

A trip to Mississippi followed where, along with Jim, Lina, and Richard, we watched Ed get his wings. The ceremony was most impressive. I now have a picture of Ed (in his plane along with a copy of his wings) on the wall of my family room. We spent the following week travelling around Mississippi. Richard came back with us to South Carolina where he was able to complete a driver training program and attend the Boy Scout National Jamboree in Virginia.

Our niece, Candace, was married in October in a beautiful outdoor wedding at the University of North Carolina. It was a joy to be with that many family members again. We sent the newly married couple off in a golf cart with sparklers lighting the darkness of the night.

Early in November, we boarded a plane in Atlanta bound for Amsterdam. The next morning, I waited at the train station for Chuck to check about our hotel. I had his new computer and our bags at my feet. A man came and asked me for change to put in a vending machine. After he left and Chuck returned, I realized our computer had gone with the man. Whether he alone took it or whether he had an accomplice, I never will know. We took the train from Amsterdam to Mannheim in Germany to attend the annual meeting of the European branch of the Counseling Association. When the conference was over, we rented a car and spent a week in the Munich area visiting Maria and Hilde, another German friend. As we had done the previous year, we flew to Lisbon, joining our friends Ginny and Al, and cruised back to Miami on the Regatta (a beautiful small cruise ship).

The year ended with our annual Christmas trip to California.

2006

Our grandson Ed was transferred to Tyndall Air Force Base in January. There, he began his training to be an F-15 fighter pilot. Chuck decided to contact a large Presbyterian church near the base to see if they would welcome him if he chose to attend. Chuck had gotten a list of the churches from our minister. Ed did decide to attend, joined the choir, and began to help with the youth group. Also helping with the youth group was a young woman, Morgan McDaniel. The two began dating. We had driven down to Panama City to see Ed's new "bachelor pad" and were invited to join Ed and Morgan for an evening of music and dancing. This was their first "official" date. Morgan's grandmother accompanied us. A couple of months later, Ed let us know that they wanted to get married. At that point, Jim, Lina, and Richard joined us in Florida to meet Morgan's family. We spent a wonderful week together.

While Ed was getting settled in Florida and we were home, we received an invitation to go to the College of Charleston (Chuck's alma mater) where he was named a "distinguished graduate." There had only been six dozen people so named since the college's founding in 1770. He received this honor because of his 46-year career as a psychologist and educator. He felt this was one of the highest honors of his life. He was given a beautiful picture of the college as a remembrance.

Chuck Latimer was honored as a distinguished alumnus of the College of Charleston in 2006.

Chuck and I had always wanted to go to Egypt. We heard of a two-week tour and decided we would take advantage of it. Many of our friends felt it was dangerous and that we shouldn't go. We did go and found it to be one of the most interesting places we had ever been. To glimpse the pyramids and tombs created prior to the time of Christ was unforgettable. We were always guarded with police escorts, and safety wasn't a problem.

Our tour guide was a certified Egyptologist who really knew her country and its history. We learned that there was a highly developed civilization in Egypt in the year 4000 B.C. No other country in the world has such a long unbroken history. We visited the Museum of Egyptian Antiquities to see the treasures of King Tutankhamen. Great beauty and opulence were before our eyes.

We flew to Luxor and visited the Karnak Temple, where we saw the tallest obelisk in Egypt made of pink granite. It was raised by Queen Hatshepsut and stands 100 feet high. We also visited Luxor temple, which was rediscovered about a century ago. It had been buried under sand and debris. We next had a cocktail cruise on a felucca (a traditional broad-sail boat used for thousands of years on the Nile).

We took a motorboat to the West Bank of the Nile. Sitting on beautiful carpets, we had breakfast served to us while we watched the boats ply the Nile. After breakfast, we visited two families. Their houses had little furniture other than beds and benches. As is done in parts of Europe, a new floor is added to the house whenever needed for the next generation. We saw turkeys and pigeons on the roofs of many houses.

We visited the Valley of the Kings where the tombs were colorfully decorated and had ramps built up to the entrance to make walking easier. While in the area, we saw the Luxor Museum where there were statues from the court of Amenhotep III. These statues have only recently been found. The museum, though small, had all the relics well displayed.

We got aboard a riverboat and stopped first at Esna, where I bought a black dress with a painting of Cleopatra on the front.

The morning after, we boarded the Nile riverboat and went to Edfu, home to the best preserved temple in Egypt.

It had only been open a short time for visitors and workers were still cleaning it while we were there. It dates back to 200 B.C.—during the time of Alexander the Great. Later, we went to Kom Ombo, which is a Nubian-style village with brightly colored houses, orange groves, and sugar cane fields.

The following day, we visited a double temple at Kom Ombo. It has one side dedicated to Sobek, the crocodile god, and the other to Haroeris, the falcon god. Medicine had been dispensed at this temple. Formulas for the medicines were carved on the temple walls. In the afternoon, we arrived at Aswan and boarded a felucca to glimpse the Mausoleum of Mohammed Shah Aga Khan and to stop on Kitchener's Island at the Botanical Gardens.

We left our riverboat the next day and took a tour of Aswan and the Philae temples. These temples were dismantled and reassembled on Agilkia Island between 1972 and 1980. The building of the high dam had threatened to submerge them completely. They had been saved by an international rescue mission sponsored by UNESCO.

While we were in this area, small boats would come alongside our boat with natives trying to sell us Egyptian clothing. One of our fellow passengers would yell over the side of the boat that she wanted to see what they were selling. A man would slip a garment into a plastic bag and throw it up to her. She'd remove it from the bag and hold it up to see if it would fit. She'd then replace the item in the bag and throw it back to the man. This was repeated several times. I don't recall her ever buying any item.

Merchants in the water in Egypt

The eleventh day of our trip, we took a felucca from Aswan to the Monastery of St. Simeon. This is a sixth century structure in the desert, and is an early Christian site. To get there, we had to ride a camel. Getting on a camel is not easy. The camels had a type of saddle but no place to put one's feet. When the camel stood up, I kept sliding down his neck, especially going downhill, and there were many. It was very hot, and we had to wear thin cotton cloths on our heads. I am glad that camel transportation isn't the only means of getting around. I find a little goes a long way for me.

We visited the site and returned to our felucca. Getting off the camel was harder than getting on. The camel goes down forward and lastly, his rump goes down with a bump. My back didn't take the bump well, and I suffered later.

We returned to Cairo by plane and that evening joined an Egyptian family for dinner at their condo.

The following day, we were driven to Saqqara, which

A camel ride in Egypt

is south of Giza. We visited the Step Pyramid of King Zoser, built in 2700 B.C. It is believed to be the first pyramid built in Egypt and is 200 feet tall. Murals inside the temple depict everyday Egyptian life.

The afternoon of the same day we were taken to see the Great Pyramids of Giza and the Sphinx. We saw the Great Pyramid of Cheops built around 2600 B.C. and nearby an ancient boat which was discovered in 1954. It is the world's oldest planked vessel, which was buried at the foot of the Great Pyramid in order to carry the pharaoh's mummy across the Nile to Memphis. The 144-foot long boat – perfectly preserved – was made of cedar with wooden dowels and battens, but no nails.

Our last day in Cairo, we drove through the Islamic quarters of the city and went to the Citadel, a medieval fortress where we had a view of Old Cairo. Later, we visited the bazaar where I purchased some beautiful Egyptian shawls. In the evening, we had front row seats at a sound and light show at the pyramids. It was a wonderful ending to a fascinating trip. To see pyramids still standing after so many years and think of all the history that has taken place since their creation was awe-inspiring.

We flew home and entertained our friend, Jacque, who was attending a medical convention in Atlanta. After he left, Richard came to be with us for the summer. We had planned to go to Germany and Croatia with Richard, but in early June, I stepped out of the shower, put my leg on a bench to dry it, and a stabbing pain shot through my back. X-rays and an MRI showed I had a stenosis and herniated discs in my back. I had six weeks of physical therapy, epidural injections, and acupuncture. I sat many days with an ice pack on my back to relieve the pain. Needless to say, we didn't go to Europe.

When I was able and could go in the car, we took Richard to see colleges he thought he was interested in attending. We visited Georgia Tech, the University of South Carolina, Duke, MIT, RPI, and Cornell. As it turned out, he didn't choose any of them, but decided to go to Rice

The Step Pyramid

University (his dad's alma mater).

Ed was to go to England after he finished his F-15 training. He and Morgan decided it would be best to get married before he left so she could accompany him. They set the date for September 7. This date was our fifty-ninth wedding anniversary and Jim and Lina's twenty-seventh anniversary. Since Jim and Lina had so recently been in Florida and had no more leave time, they couldn't attend. Richard was back at college.

The wedding took place in Morgan's church, Grace Presbyterian, with her pastor officiating. A small reception followed, hosted by her grandfather. A larger reception was held in October at Tyndal AFB for a large number of family and friends. After their wedding, Ed and Morgan went to a condo on Panama City Beach for a couple of days. Ed called us and said the condo had two bedrooms with adjoining baths. He wondered if we could join them. We did and enjoyed sharing our meals with them. Chuck liked to say there weren't many grandchildren who would invite their grandparents to share their honeymoon suite.

Getting Morgan to accompany Ed to England was a trial. Morgan needed a government passport and a resident visa to allow her to live in England. The passport office on the base was run by a woman who only worked a couple of days a week and was in no way helpful. She said it might take several months to get a passport. Chuck finally contacted our senator here, and his office got the passport almost immediately. When Ed told the woman on base they didn't need her service, she looked at him and replied, "Oh shit!"

Once she had her passport, Morgan contacted a courier in Washington to get her British visa. It arrived two days before they were to leave. When Chuck looked at it, he noticed the visa in the passport stated the date of issue and the date it was no longer valid as the same date. In other words, it was good for less than one day. The passport had to be sent back for correction, and the new one arrived the morning they were to leave. It reminded us of Jim and Lina's passport problem years before.

After much packing and stress, they finally got to England and found a new four-bedroom home to rent in Thetford. This was the town one of Chuck's ancestors had helped to establish many years before. We were later to visit the ruins of the abbey he had built.

Our Thanksgiving holiday was spent in California with Jim and Lina, and they, along with Richard, spent Christmas with us.

Mary no longer needed to go to the workshop after a psychiatrist declared it was not benefitting her. She was no longer anxious each day as she had been when she had to face a noisy workshop.

2007

In early January, we flew to England to visit Ed and Morgan. One weekend, we all went to London to visit the Tower of London, Paddington Station, and to see the changing of the guards at Buckingham Palace. We also visited April and Charles at their apartment in Chelsea. We stayed at a small hotel on the outskirts of London.

After visiting in Thetford, we flew to Munich and saw Maria and Hilde for a couple of days. When we returned to England, we borrowed Ed and Morgan's car and drove to Stotfold to see Jane and Peter and their children. When we got to Stotfold, we became confused about how to reach their home. We got on a street with trucks parked on both sides of the road. Chuck thought he could get between the trucks, but we scraped the truck and Ed's car. The truck company filed for damages about a year later, and in the report, the date and place of the accident were incorrect. However, our insurance company paid the bill. We had Ed's car repaired, but it was never the same. I think we learned it's best to rent a car and not to borrow one from a family member.

We returned home and enjoyed a Greenville spring with its many activities, including the Panama Canal Reunion in Florida. However, we returned to Europe again in April and flew to Venice, where we spent a few days before getting on the M/S Dalmacija, a Croatian ship, which plied along the Adriatic Coast. There were eight of us Americans, and the rest of the passengers were German. I really got to use my speaking German. This was the trip we didn't get to take in 2006.

In Venice, we spent the days using the ferries, which go through the canals, and walking through the city. Since neither Chuck nor I could walk far, we'd stop and find a place to sit. We never knew what we'd find around the next corner. Once, we found a man singing opera. He played a cassette and sang along with it. Another time, there was a mime artist dressed in a silver costume. We came to a big square with outdoor restaurants on all sides. Near us was a fountain with a basin at the bottom to catch the water. Birds flew into the basin to bathe. A couple with two small boys was sitting at a nearby table drinking wine. One of the boys came and began playing in the water. His mother got up, came over, and took him away from the water. She returned to the table and continued to talk and drink. In a short while, the boy was back with both feet in the water. By the time his mother realized what was happening, he was completely soaked. We had to leave at that point so I don't know whether his clothes got changed or he just stayed wet.

We left Venice past Piazzi San Marcos early on Saturday morning, April 7 (the day before Easter). We arrived in Zadar the following morning. The ship was small and was able to pull up at each city's main dock. Since it was Easter, we tried to go to Saint Donat's Church, but it was so crowded, we stood outside to hear the service. Following church, we walked by the Roman Forum on the way back to our ship.

Our next stop was Ploce where we took a tour to Mostar, which has minarets, houses with wooden balconies, and an old bridge built in 1566. This area was under the Ottoman rule for centuries.

Korcula Island was our subsequent stop. Legend says this island was settled by the Trojan hero Anthenos in the twelfth century B.C. A statute signed in 1214 A.D. prohibited the slave trade. Marco Polo was supposed to have been here. We were shown the house in which he was supposedly born.

After Korcula we visited Kotor, a UNESCO "World Heritage Site." It dates back to the twelfth and fourteenth centuries and has medieval architecture. The streets are narrow and lead to many squares.

We stopped in Dubrovnik (formerly Ragusa). We had been there before but enjoyed once more seeing this beautiful city with its cathedral, Rector's Palace, old monastery, and city walls.

When we reached Pula, I was amazed to see a huge Roman amphitheater built back in the second century B.C. near the port. In Julius Caesar's time, this was a flourishing town. There is a Roman Forum, a temple of Augustus, and two gates dating back to the first and second century B.C. The amphitheater is the sixth largest monument of its kind the world.

Our last port of call before Venice was Koper. This city is on the Gulf of Trieste. From here, we chose to visit the Cave of Postojna. These are the most visited caves in Europe. More than three million people have visited them since they were opened to the public 85 years ago. We rode on a cave train that took us all through the cave. The scenery in the cave was spectacular. The cave had been studied by scientists as early as the seventeenth century.

The whole cruise was interesting and made one realize how far the Roman Empire had extended. We returned to Venice and flew up to England to be with Ed and Morgan. While with Morgan, I enjoyed visiting the farm markets with their fresh produce, cheeses, and frozen foods.

In July, Morgan joined Chuck and me for a Baltic cruise. We cruised on the Norwegian Dream. Our ship had a retractable smoke stack. Apparently, it was the only

Chuck and Alice Latimer celebrated their sixtieth wedding anniversary on board the Norwegian Dream in 2007.

ship with this design, and this was its last voyage before it was taken out of service. Because the stack could be folded down, we were able to go through the Kiel Canal. We could stand at the rail and watch mothers pushing baby carriages, people biking, and folks walking their dogs. Many smiled and waved to us.

We stopped at Warnemünde, rented a car, and visited Schwerin and the area above Berlin. We had never been there before, as it was still part of East Germany when we lived in Europe. The area was beautiful with many castles and historic buildings.

Our next stop was Helsinki and then St. Petersburg. We had been to Helsinki before and didn't take a tour. However, we enjoyed a city tour of St. Petersburg, a ride on the canals, and a visit to the cathedral of Spilled Blood. The artwork inside the cathedral was magnificent. The colors were vivid reds, blues, and greens, all offset with gold. I stood there in awe, wondering how much money it must have taken to build such a church.

We left St. Petersburg and stopped at: Tallinn, Estonia; Stockholm, Sweden; and Copenhagen, Denmark before returning to Dover. We got off the ship at each of these ports and walked about near the ship. We had been to each of these cities before. The one thing I regret was that I didn't visit the Hermitage in St. Petersburg. I was told one had to walk and stand for about three hours. I knew I was just not up to that type of a tour. I'd have to look at a book of the rooms instead.

My cousin, Randy, came to Thetford one weekend from Sheffield, where he had been working. He enjoyed watching Ed fly. The F-15 planes take off with a roar.

We were in England in September, where we celebrated our sixtieth wedding anniversary. Tom and Connie had come to England from Australia and joined us for lunch at a restaurant in Thetford. They had been with us on our fiftieth anniversary and wanted to be with us again. Ed and Morgan chose not to go with us for lunch but instead went to Bath to celebrate their anniversary.

We came back home after our anniversary and were here until November when we took a cruise from Charleston to Bermuda. We enjoyed our time on Bermuda and took many pictures. We played the "Newlywed" and "Not-so-Newlywed" game one night, and as a result, people stopped and chatted with us. Many were surprised we had been married 60 years.

The seas were very rough on the way back. The waves crested at 26 or 27 feet. As we came back, the Bermuda Rescue Center contacted our ship to go to the aid of a person in a sailboat who needed immediate medical attention. The ship turned around and went to the aid of the individual. We stood at the rail of the ship watching the lights on the boat as we got near. The seas were so rough and the wind so strong that the sailboat couldn't be brought alongside our ship. We watched as a launch was put down with a crew, including a doctor. The ill person was brought aboard our ship, placed in the infirmary, and taken back to Charleston. We were never told what the problem was.

Because we had lost time with the emergency, and because of an engine problem, we were a day late getting back home. No one had service charges on the last day and everyone got to make a free telephone call or use the Internet. The ship was almost out of food but was able to serve us breakfast. Some people were annoyed at getting back late. One lady missed her grandson's wedding. We just enjoyed the extra sea day.

We ended the year with a visit to California after Christmas. Ed and Morgan joined us for New Year's. They came with English snappers, used in England for Christmas. When we opened them, out fell tiny toy babies, rattles, and baby bottles. Chuck was first to guess what this meant. We were going to be great grandparents! We were thrilled.

2008

Little did I know at the beginning of this year that my life would be greatly changed by the end of it. I would be a widow. Somehow, I think Chuck had a feeling he might not live long. He made me promise that this year I'd go wherever he wanted to go and do whatever he wanted to do. I agreed to his wishes.

Chuck loved cruising. While we were in California, he said he wanted to go to the Mexican Riviera. We found a cruise that went to Cabo San Lucas, Puerto Vallarta, Zihuatanejo, and Acapulco before returning to Los Angeles. There was a colorful Mexican folkloric show one night with prehistoric dances. We enjoyed both the music and dance.

In early spring, the American Counseling meeting was held in Hawaii. We flew to Hawaii and spent three weeks there. We were on Oahu, Kauai, and the big island of Hawaii. One of the highlights of our trip was a visit to an orchid grower's greenhouse. I have always loved orchids and was amazed to see the many varieties and colors. Some of the blooms were huge. I wished I could carry some home.

Chuck wanted to go to England again to see Ed and Morgan. We decided to go with a cruise. We left Ft. Lauderdale and stopped at the beautiful Madeira Island,

Sardinia, Rome, and France. In Madeira, we went to Monte and the Church of Our Lady of the Mountain. It is here one can see the tomb of Emperor Charles V of Austria. Just below the church down a steep set of steps, there were men selling rides on straw toboggans. Madeira has many hills, and one can go a long way on the toboggans. We had never been to Sardinia before. I didn't realize it was so hilly. I was amazed to find an elevator in the middle of the main city to enable people to get from one level of the town to another.

In Rome, we walked around a bit and saw the Vatican from a distance. We simply weren't up to waiting in line to visit the Sistine Chapel or other attractions. We remembered many years before when we had been there at Easter and had seen the Pope.

After we landed in Barcelona, we flew to France. It was springtime and the lilac and chestnut trees were in bloom. The blend of the white candle-like blossoms of the chestnut trees with the purple of the lilacs trees makes for beautiful landscapes. Crops had been planted, and fields were green or yellow with rapeseed. We took the train and visited our friends in Lyon and Auxerre and then spent time in Bourges with Jacques and his wife. We left France and visited a couple of weeks with Ed and Morgan, then flew home.

We attended Richard's high school graduation in June. Ed flew from England to join us. We were so proud of Richard, as he was named a Centennial Scholar at Rice University where he would start classes in the fall. It is always nice to have an occasion for our family to be

Richard Latimer's graduation from Palos Verdes Peninsula
High School in California

---

together, and this was such an occasion. The fact that both
Ed and Richard had spent summers with us made us feel
very close to both grandsons.

The Canal Zone reunion is always in early July. We
drove down and had the opportunity to visit many old
friends. Each year, there is a memorial surfing event in
remembrance of some young men who died prematurely
of cancer. One of these was David, the son of our friends
the Paynes. We attended that event and saw former
students. We also visited my cousins in De Land and our
friends the Murphys.

When August came, Chuck said, "Let's drive to Boston
and see the places where we lived and where we dated."
We stopped in Englewood and saw my old home and the
church where we were married. We stayed Hanscom Air
Base near Boston and visited Lexington and Concord. We
ate at the Wayside Inn where we used to go on special
occasions.

We drove to Cape Cod and visited my high school

friend Helen. On the way, we stopped to see Val, my college roommate. We had stopped in Connecticut on the way to see Chuck's cousins and enjoyed a fish fry with them. We took a cruise from Boston to Canada. We visited St. John's, Newfoundland, Halifax, Nova Scotia, and Bangor, Maine. Our former Canal Zone friends, the Bakers, were at the pier to meet us in Bangor. We spent the day with them going to Arcadia National Park. It was a day spent remembering the good times when we had been together. We stopped and ate lobster, a real treat! That night, on the boat, we celebrated our sixty-first wedding anniversary.

We got home on a Tuesday. The next day, Chuck went around the neighborhood telling everyone about our journey. He was especially pleased that he had been able to drive us up to Boston and back. I, of course, was the navigator. That day, we received word that our great grandson, Samuel Laurens Latimer, had been born in England. A picture of Sam was on the computer.

The following morning, a Thursday, about 4 a.m., I awoke to hear a strange sound. It was Chuck trying to tell me something, but I couldn't understand him. He had suffered a massive stroke. I called EMS, and an ambulance came to take him to the hospital. I followed. Jim and Lina came quickly, and Ed flew from England. Chuck died Friday night – two and a half hours short of his eighty-fourth birthday. He had enjoyed the entire year and knew there was a new baby in the family. We had been together 61 years. He didn't need anything more.

A wonderful memorial service was put on in our church with bagpipes playing "Amazing Grace" and "Taps" played by bugle. Chuck was so proud of his Scotch-Irish heritage and would have wanted the bagpipes. Both Jim and Ed spoke, as did Clarence Payne, our former minister in the Canal Zone. Clarence and his wife Rosita then stayed for few days with me. Ed also stayed with me for about a week. There had been a hurricane in Texas, which prevented Richard from coming, but he sent his remarks about his grandpa. Morgan and Sam came later from England and stayed with me for a week.

Chuck always told me I was a strong person as well as one who could adjust to whatever came along. He said, "If anything happens to me and I die first, you must go on with your life. If you find another man to love, I give you permission to love him. I will always remember the love you have shown to me and the blessing of 61 years together." I have remembered his words.

I spent the Thanksgiving after Chuck's death in Florida with Morgan and her family. Before Christmas, Ed and Dot, along with Mary and Lewis (Chuck's cousins) joined me at Myrtle Beach for some Christmas shows. Jim, Lina, and Richard joined Mary and me for Christmas. Mary has accepted her dad's death well. She says, "He is in heaven."

Rosita Payne, left, wife of minister Clarence Payne, with
Alice Latimer and friend Millie in Greenville

Greenville, SC friends

Living Alone

In my training as a counselor, I learned the value of support groups. When one loses a partner, there is a need to find someone else with whom to share one's feelings and problems. My doctor, after Chuck's death, asked if I needed any medication to help deal with my grief. She also suggested my going to a grief group. I said I didn't need any medication, and I haven't gone to a grief group.

In the days after Chuck's passing, I was kept busy filling out forms, getting rid of his clothes, and going through his papers. I'm still sorting through those papers after three years.

My friends have been a blessing. Millie calls me every day to see if I'm all right. She came into my life when she first arrived in Greenville. Her husband had left on a business trip before they had gotten unpacked. Our former minister, Clarence, had been her minister when she lived in Washington D.C. He suggested she call us when she reached Greenville and that we would help her. She called, came to supper, and we have been friends ever since.

Other friends, Ethel, Ginny, Mia, Carol, and Kwang – and my church circle of friends – are there for me when I need them. We go out to eat together and share holiday meals.

Friends Maria Krull Buchholz and Dee Miller in
Garmisch in 2009

I have continued with my former activities, although
I'm not getting to the night meetings because I no longer
drive at night and need someone to take me to these.

One of the first things I did was to check my house to
make sure it was safe for me to live alone. I have an alarm
system on the house, which gives me peace of mind at
night. I wear a button around my neck in case of a fall. I
also had my bathroom made into a handicapped bath,
which means I don't have to step over the side of the tub
anymore.

My friend Millie belongs to the Commerce Club. She
called one night to say that another lady at the club, Sondra
(whom we call the "Match Maker") wanted to know if I'd
go to a concert with a widower if he called. I said I'd be
happy to. There, I met Dick who has been a blessing to
me. He is a kind, warm individual with many talents

different from Chuck's. We each live in our own homes but see each other daily; especially, we eat dinner together. We also enjoy travelling together.

In October of 2009, we flew to Denver and visited Dick's two sons. We drove to Rocky Mountain National Park and stayed two nights at the Stanley Hotel, which is over 100 years old. A Stanley Steamer sits in the lobby and is in workable condition. A wedding was taking place that afternoon, and a pulpit and chairs had been placed on the lawn facing the mountains. I thought what a beautiful place to be married. The bride and her party were having their pictures taken on the staircase leading to the lobby.

We had gone to the park to see the elk rutting (mating). The males lock horns and make deep noises. We saw many elk, but no actual rutting. In one part of the park, we got caught in a snowstorm. It was so cold, we hurried back to our car. The mountains were beautiful, some snow-capped,

Alice Latimer and Dick Lambrecht

and the day was clear. We ended up at a fair, perched ourselves on a window ledge and each had an ice cream cone. The temperature was cold, but we enjoyed our cones.

In the early fall of 2009, Ed was transferred to Shaw Air Force Base in South Carolina. I was delighted they would be near me. Dick and I have spent many days with them since they have returned from England.

Knowing they were returning to the States, I decided to book a cruise to Amsterdam in order to visit them one last time in Europe. Chuck had put down some money for a cruise, and I had never used the certificate. Dee Miller, a friend from the Reserve Officers Wives group, went with me. She had lost her husband a year before Chuck died.

Our ship stopped in the Madeira Islands, Spain, France, and England before reaching Amsterdam. Dee had never been in Paris, and this gave her an opportunity to go there. I had always wanted to go to Giverny to see Monet's garden, which he made famous through his paintings. I couldn't have chosen a better time to see the flowers in bloom. There were tulips, forget-me-nots, wisteria, azaleas, poppies, and roses. Weeping willows were reflected in the ponds. A green arched trellis was draped with purple wisteria. We walked over a bridge under the wisteria. The sweet odor of flowers followed wherever we went. The tour to Giverny was followed by a delicious lunch at a French inn by a millpond. In Amsterdam, we visited the Ann Frank house. There was a large crowd waiting to go through the house, but we waited patiently because we both felt it was something we wanted to see. We left the house wondering whether we could have lived as that family had, hidden away.

In July, my friend Millie and I decided to take a cruise to Alaska. I had been there before, but Millie hadn't. We stood at the rail and watched pieces of glaciers break off and plunge into the sea. Water splashed upward for many feet, and there was a tremendous roar. We also saw one moose, humpback whales, and puffins, along with many beautiful flowers. I recalled that many years before, my aunt returned from a trip to Alaska and described how tall the flowering plants were.

In Vancouver, we docked and enjoyed seeing Butchart Gardens and the beautiful waterfront with its hotels and shops.

At Furman University, there is a program called OLLI (Osher Lifelong Learning Institute). Dick had been going there for several years and suggested I join him. Volunteers staff the program and offer a variety of courses on various topics. There are three terms in a year – fall is 10 weeks, while winter and spring are eight weeks. There was a short summer term added in 2011. I have joined him there. Two times a week, we eat breakfast at the Commerce Club, then attend class, and have lunch at the university. I have found the classes stimulating and the people friendly and intelligent.

Last year, 2010, was a fulfilling one for me. In March, Dick and I took a cruise to the Caribbean. We stopped at the Dominican Republic, Antigua, the British Virgin Islands, St. Kitts, and Barbados. Although I had been there before, Dick had never been on an ocean cruise and thoroughly enjoyed it. At the end of the cruise, we visited

Dick and Alice vacationing in Wisconsin

some of Dick's family in Florida and South Carolina.

Dick's hobby is building miniature steam engines. He belongs to the American Model Engineering Society, which meets yearly near Detroit. We have attended their convention both last year and this year. We took the occasion last year to visit the Henry Ford Greenfield Village and Museum. We were able to rent little motorized carts both at the museum and at the village itself to enable us to traverse the entire area. This allowed us to see everything. With little walking, we saw the Wright brothers' workshop and Henry Ford's boyhood home.

Many of Dick's family and friends live in the Midwest. It is an area with which I'm not familiar. Last summer we drove to Wisconsin from Greenville, stopping along the way to visit people whom Dick has known. We spent the first night at the Shaker Colony near Lexington, Kentucky. We stayed in one of the Shaker buildings, which was attractive but sparsely furnished. Pegs were on the wall to hold one's clothing. Pegs were also used to hold extra chairs in the dining room. While in Wisconsin, I had a chance to ride on a dirt bike and a motorcycle. I had never ridden either before.

My cousins Jenny and Phil have a summer home on a Wisconsin lake. I had not seen them in a number of years. We visited them for two days before coming home. It was a happy reunion. Dick and Phil enjoyed chatting together. Phil, a physician, shared his stories, and Dick spoke of his inventions.

Last year was a fulfilling one for Jim as well. As I have mentioned earlier, he is an electrical engineer. While he worked at Hughes, he designed the antennas for some of the satellites. For the past 10 years, he had been working on a satellite. In the fall of 2010, he participated in the successful launch of this satellite. He was thrilled to sit at the console and watch it take off and go into orbit.

Richard is currently in his senior year at Rice University. He loves his studies there and plans to stay to complete his master's degree. He spent one semester last year at the National University of Singapore. While there, he had a chance to fly both to Indonesia and Australia to visit his mother's family.

Ed spent six months last year in Afghanistan as part of the ISAF (International Security Assistance Force) with the Italian and German armies. He was in the north of the country at the foot of the Hindu Kush Mountains. He has been transferred to Pope Army Airfield in North Carolina. He and Morgan are looking forward to the arrival of their second child in early December. This new baby will join brother Sam who just celebrated his third birthday.

This year, I have not been travelling. My back gave me

a lot of pain during the winter. I began physical therapy and then had acupuncture. A few days after having an acupuncture treatment, I developed a rash on my side, which I attributed to the treatment. When the rash began to spread, Millie and her husband David drove me to the emergency room. There, the doctor told me I had shingles. I had pain and itching for six weeks and had no energy at all. I just wanted to lie down and rest. Now, I'm better and my energy has returned. I'm eager to pack up and get under way. Thursday of this week, I'll board a plane with Dick to head to Rome and a Mediterranean cruise. We especially look forward to seeing the Sistine Chapel, other parts of the Vatican, and the statue of David in Florence.

Writing My Story

In order to write my memoirs, I have had to rely on Christmas letters that Chuck wrote each year and notes about trips that we both wrote. I always wanted Chuck to write about our life and travels because he was an excellent writer, better than I am. Unfortunately, his stroke prevented this from happening. I have enjoyed this past year as I have spent time reliving so many wonderful memories. Psychologists say we should all do this before the end of our lives to see if we have any unfinished business. God has blessed me with a wonderful supportive husband, an attentive and loving family, and now a loving friend and companion. How lucky can one woman be!

A course, which I took at Furman with instructor Amanda Capps, who later became my editor, made me realize I needed to write this book to share my life with friends and family. I hope those of you who have read these stories enjoyed them. I hope you too will take all the opportunities that come your way to travel, to learn about different cultures, and to realize that in this world, people are basically alike, and that we all have the same needs.

My story ends as it began, with a cruise to see some of the wonders of this beautiful world. My journey has had mountains to climb and valleys to cross, but at each one, I have had the will and the strength to forge ahead. I look forward to whatever may come in my future. I dedicate this book to my family and my friends who have enriched my life. May you all enjoy your lives as I have and be able to say: "If I had to live life over, I'd do it the same way."

Alice received the Pioneer Award from the S.C. Counseling Association. She is pictured with her grandson Ed, his wife Morgan, and their son Sammy.

"Crossing's End"

Dear friends, come help me mourn the loss
Of this the only way to cross
And please, can anyone forefend
The specter of our journey's end?

It seems a year since boarding pass
Since baggage tag and champagne glass
Since whistle's blast and engine thrill
Since *Bon Voyage* and lifeboat drill

Since stewardess and breakfast tray
And all those things we stowed away
To bring: that awful chore
We'd never do on either shore

But shipboard's most seductive thread
PROCRASTINATION—ruled instead.
The miles we've walked, the drinks we've drunk
The food we gorged, the clothes we shrunk!

Now, gulls have found us far at sea

The Purser's done with you and me

And everything we try and pack

Requires an extra haversack

Tomorrow, we'll awake oppressed

With tugs outside as we get dressed

What tugs at me is, quite befitting

The gloom of "Breakfast, Final Sitting"

Enough—it's time to come to grips

To part with friends and handsome trips

To wait until "The Ship is Cleared!"

(That haunting phrase, both cheered and feared)

"Goodbye!" "Farewell!" "We'll see you soon!"

But, sadly, by mid-afternoon

A new and faceless horde

Displaces us as souls on board

A month from now, enjoy and laugh

Examining any photograph

And wife or husband will exclaim:

"There's you with Captain What's-his-name!"

John Maxtone-Graham

The journey continues . . .

Afterword

Grandma,

As I read your book, I truly realized what a great storyteller you are!

Although I had heard many of the stories before (some more than a few times), I had many chuckles while reading about your childhood and your time in Germany and Panama. Once I got to the chapters about our adventures in South America and Europe, I recalled many fond memories from those summer trips. Some that came to mind included my working as a bellhop in our hotel in Istanbul, Turkey, losing you as I ran ahead to cool down the car in Assisi, Italy, racing up the mountainside while calling you and Grandpa "over the hill" in Slovakia, accidentally waking Grandpa and you early in the morning for my first driving lesson in France, fishing for piranha on the Amazon outside Manaus, Brazil, visiting a nightclub in Rio de Janeiro, seeing Iguazu Falls in Argentina, attending a day of Welsh school in Wales, and getting attacked by a four-foot cactus in Göttingen, Germany – among many others!

After spending so much time with you during the summers, I really felt your home was a "home away from home," especially after I moved off to college. Grandpa and you visited many times both while I was stateside and after Morgan and I moved to England. Even now, after Grandpa's passing, Dick and you have continued to visit us. We are very thankful that your mind is still sharp and that you are in good health and continue to travel. I thank you for giving Morgan and me the "travel bug" and for writing your memoirs.

May you have many more adventures!

Ed Latimer

Editor's Note

What a joy it has been to travel around the world with Alice Latimer. In addition to reading of her adventures, I have delighted in her sense of accomplishment. Alice has become an informal ambassador for memoir writing and has already inspired others to take on similar projects. She has shown her editor, her family, and her friends that this type of book helps writers appreciate their own achievements and blessings from a completely new perspective. It also allows future generations to hear your voice and to mark history. Whether you need a ghost writer, an editor – or just a good listener, please contact me if you'd like to chronicle your journey.

Amanda Capps

AMANDA INK
GREENVILLE, SOUTH CAROLINA
864-363-1528
AMANDACAPPSINK@GMAIL.COM